MW01633715

Beating Bad Breath
THE CURE©

Your Complete Guide to
Preventing, Treating, and Curing Halitosis

Richard A. Miller, DDS
Director, National Breath Center

ISBN Number   978-0-9895027-0-2

National Breath Center
Falls Church, VA

Printed in the United States of America

A NEW BEGINNING FOR THOSE
WITH BAD BREATH

My goal and the purpose for this book is to help free you from the worries and fears of bad breath and to help bring CONFIDENCE back into your life. **For those of you who have these concerns, please know that:**

1. **You Are Not Alone.**

   In over 22 years, I have seen over 7,000 people with all levels of halitosis—people socially incapacitated, social lives ruined, weddings called off, engagements broken, jobs lost, and even divorce. This is why I expanded and rewrote my original book, *Beating Bad Breath* (1995) — for others to know that there is help. Help that works. And ***this book is the latest revised edition of the 2013 edition.***

2. **Halitosis is a true condition that can be CURED, even if medicine and dentistry do not see it as such.**

   For over 22 years, I have treated people with a 100% cure rate. This book will give you much of the knowledge I have accumulated about CLINICAL and AT HOME treatment and help you find what works for you.

Richard A. Miller DDS

National Breath Center

7115 Leesburg Pike   Suite 309

Falls Church, VA 22043

www.beathalitosis.com

INTRODUCTION

Imagine meeting new people who offer you gum or mints, cover their noses, or stand back. Imagine your dates turning their cheek away just as you go to kiss them, people who move back a step when you are close enough to breathe on them, or co-workers who do all of the above. And, imagine your husband or wife not wanting to kiss you because of your breath. Imagine having that fear all the time. This is what people with halitosis go through every day. I see the fear in their faces when they come in as a new person to our office. I hear their skepticism when told I can cure them and I listen to their stories, most always with unhappy circumstances devastating to their confidence and their lives.

There is a CURE! A TOTAL CURE!

I know because I have personally treated and cured over 7,000 patients with halitosis since 1993. And the people I see at the National Breath Center come from all over the world – 27 countries including the Middle East, Philippines, England, Japan, Africa, Europe and almost every state in the U.S.

In 1995, my first book, *Beating Bad Breath,* was published—the only published book on treating bad breath at that time. Since then, I have taught thousands of dentists at 9 major dental meetings in the U.S. and Europe, and in 22 all-day seminars across the country.

As I continued to cure thousands of people with halitosis over the last 20 years, from mild to the most severe case imaginable, the doctors I taught seem to have forgotten the cure and the profession has turned to selling products instead of curing people. Products are certainly easier to offer as a cure, but the TOTAL CURE takes knowledge, hard work, experience, and caring.

In this book I will tell you what works, what doesn't, and why. I will present the TOTAL CURE for the thousands I have treated. I will tell you how to *maintain the TOTAL CURE indefinitely.* In addition, I will relate some of the stories I have heard over the past years and how the TOTAL CURE has affected people's lives.

Moreover, for those who cannot find a dentist who offers the TOTAL CURE, I will offer you a proven self-treatment technique – the **Beating Bad Breath Protocol**© – that will put you in control of your problem.

Richard A. Miller DDS
NATIONAL BREATH CENTER
7115 Leesburg Pike Suite 309
Falls Church, VA 22043
703-533-0927
www.beathalitosis.com

Why I specialize in curing bad breath

When I began to cure bad breath, I had been in practice for almost 20 years. During that time, I had performed almost every dental procedure possible – from surgery to advanced restorative dentistry. I had long since mastered the techniques and procedures that define a superior dentist.

However, in 1993, I began to truly change people's lives. I was able to see someone go from withdrawn and depressed to outgoing and optimistic; to save a marriage; to help weddings go forward instead of a broken engagement; to see estranged people find their love again; to help people get a job promotion; to help people who had given up hope and those who would not quit looking for a cure; and to cure someone after 35 years of their seeking a cure. This is what drives me – knowing that I am truly changing people's lives by curing their bad breath.

Sitting across from someone, hearing their story, and empathizing with their plight, occurs for me almost every day at the National Breath Center. These feelings have become a calling – to help people reclaim their normal lives by eliminating the insidious condition of chronic bad breath.

Many people I see have tried numerous bad breath cures and seek me out because they have almost no hope left; I find great satisfaction in knowing I can cure them. Curing people of bad breath is the greatest joy I could never have imagined when I entered dentistry.

Richard A. Miller DDS

TABLE OF CONTENTS

THE ROAD TO THE CURE

In mid fall of 1992, I received a phone call from a patient whom I had known since I opened my office - the mother of a bride-to-be who was to be married in March of the next year. I remember the emotion in that call as she choked back tears. Her future son-in-law had just told her daughter that he was calling off the wedding as her daughter had mouth odor he could no longer be near.

As I became a confidant to her story, the mother began asking, then pleading with me to help her daughter. I told her to have Jennifer come in the next day to see me.

Jennifer was a young woman 27 years old. As she sat in my dental chair, she related her story.

Jennifer had had an occasional bad taste in her mouth for years and even thought she might have bad breath, but she had thought nothing of it. Mouthwashes, toothpastes, or gum always seemed to take care of it even though a few people had told her about her breath problem.

Then Brian came along. After they had been dating 6 months, Brian asked her to marry him. All seemed to go well until they had been engaged for about 4 months. As she was making her wedding plans, Brian began to "avoid" her. First, she thought it was the anxiety of getting married. However, her friend Marilyn, a bridesmaid-to-be, told her the reason: Brian was turned off by her breath.

Jennifer, of course, was beside herself. She was in love with Brian and didn't want to lose him. She didn't know what to do. She came to see me since I had been her family dentist since she was a young girl.

When she told me her problem, I felt helpless. I had never read anything in the professional literature about a formal treatment for halitosis. So I began a search of all the known information about bad breath.

I spent days off and weekends at Georgetown University Medical Library studying all past research on halitosis since 1900. I copied hundreds of pages from long forgotten journals and scientific papers.

Even though I had no treatment protocol at that time, what I *did* have was a desire to help this young woman. So before she came into the office for the diagnosis, I devised some simple steps and observations for my first halitosis exam. Based on my thoughts at that time about where any odor could be coming from, my exam consisted of the following:

       Periodontal (gum disease) measurements

       Bleeding areas

       Soft tissue exam

       Check for food traps

       X-rays for decay or abscess

       Organoleptic reading (smell test)

No products had yet been invented to kill the bacteria that caused bad breath or to neutralize the odor. Nothing other than cleaning the teeth and deep cleaning, if needed, were recommended as a therapeutic regimen. So we did what was recommended in dentistry at that time and improvised other treatments. Over the course of treating Jennifer, I developed an original protocol to eliminate halitosis and went on to teach it to over 10,000 dentists in the U.S. and Europe.

Sometime before her exam, I had read about the smell (organoleptic) test for halitosis but needed to devise my own technique. For the organoleptic reading, I smelled the odor in her mouth, at 1 and 6 inches from her face. I had her expel a gentle breath of air no matter where my nose was and subjectively compared them to the one-inch reading, which I considered the baseline. Needless to say, it was not a pleasant task. I found that her fiancé really did have a point. What to do?

Since her initial treatment appointment was 4 weeks from her first visit, I began to look at things in the mouths I had previously glossed over of patients. I smelled food in food traps between the teeth; I asked patients to breathe on me at 1 and 6 inches, before they had their teeth cleaned. I asked if they had ever experienced the social signals that Jennifer had related to me. I started to see the anatomy of their tongues and their coatings; I began to look at their throat and tonsils, and I began to swab and smell their tongue coatings. I began to see possible connection, so I kept testing and observing.

Six weeks after I began treatment Jennifer came in with her fiancé in tow. We chatted for a few minutes as she worked her way to telling me her good news. She **was** getting married. I was thrilled for her, congratulated her, and decided to ask Brian a question: "What changed for you?" As best I can remember from 1993, here were his words.

"I had loved Jennifer from the moment we met in college. Her problem was minor but just noticeable then. During our engagement, I found it getting worse. I was even holding my breath when I was close. I simply started to avoid her.

'After a lot of thought, I tried to weigh how her problem would affect our lives together. I decided my only recourse would be to try to find someone else. But the thought of living without Jen was too painful. I could only hope she would find some help."

I interjected, "Have you noticed a change in her breath?" "Yes," he replied. "I no longer need to worry about being close.

'Whatever you did has allowed me to focus on more important things—like our wedding." They both smiled at each other then got up to leave. Unexpectedly, Jennifer wrapped her arms around me in a hug, and Brian shook my hand. They left the office hand in hand.

Of course, I had not yet developed the TOTAL CURE, which was two years later, but what I had done for Jennifer created no discernible bad breath – I had CURED Jennifer.

Helping Jennifer and Brian spurred me on to continuing observation and experimentation— searching for something the literature, the research, the academics, and my peers said did not exist—The Cure for Bad Breath.

PART I

CURRENT TREATMENT DOES NOT WORK

WHY CURRENT TREATMENT DOES NOT WORK

Americans spend billions of dollars annually for fresh breath. This includes mints, gums, mouthwashes, toothpastes, sprays, and numerous other products. The one characteristic these have in common is that *they only cover up the mouth odor* with a stronger, more pleasant odor that lasts a short time. That's it!

As I updated my investigation of over-the-counter (OTC) mouthwashes for this book, in most all mouthwashes the ingredients always included essential oils with strong odors, like eucalyptus oil, menthol, and mint. These are cover-ups and have little or no therapeutic ability to treat bad breath. And the ones with alcohol are even worse. Alcohol is not listed as an active ingredient, but it is obvious that the astringency of the alcohol is what we feel that makes it seem as if an antiseptic is cleaning our mouths.

In 1992, *Consumer Reports* tested the efficacy of 15 mouthwashes that claimed to eliminate bad breath, most still on the market today. Their tests found that while all mouthwashes tested were still working 10 minutes after use only some lasted more than one hour—and those only partially. *Consumer Reports* concluded, "…the results varied too greatly from person to person to generalize; no product proved to be consistently better than any other… at the end of two hours, they all had fairly little residual effect."

An old test? Yes. However, the ingredients have changed little since then Which is the reason Consumer Reports has not repeated the test; and from experience at the National

Breath Center, I would definitely agree. *Over-the-counter (OTC) mouthwashes and toothpastes do not work.*

THE WORST BREATH EVER!

One day in 1998, a man walked into my office surrounded by his wife and two daughters. By his body language, it was easy to see that he did not want to be there. Upon later questioning, he had been brought to the office by the three women who came with him and who corrected any comments he made.

After filling out the paperwork- medical history, dental history, and our halitosis questionnaire- he was brought into the treatment room at the end of the hall. This dental treatment room was about 10 feet by 12 feet in size. As I entered the room, I was able to smell his breath before the entry door - 12 feet away! I did not put on a mask as it would not have worked anyway. I proceeded in, took my seat, and began to talk with him and his entourage.

One daughter told how many people had said he had terrible breath. His wife talked about how no one would sit near him in church. They all said how bad it was being indoors with him in a closed space.

I began my investigation. He had all the symptoms and signs of severe halitosis. His tongue had a large, thick, and yellow-brown coating; he had severe gum disease, and the open contacts and food traps made it appear that his oral hygiene was nonexistent.

The Halimeter, which measures the amount of volatile sulfur compounds (VSCs) in the breath, the actual odor of halitosis, was the last instrument I used in diagnosis. The range of VSCs that can be measured is from 0-1999. When tested with the Halimeter, he registered 1999 within 30 seconds, most likely because the machine could not go any higher.

His wife and I agreed on treatment and with his nod, he showed he would do it. Over the next four months, we cured his breath problem. The Halimeter readings had come down to 100. At the end of his treatment, I felt I had accomplished something unique.

He had been aloof from the time I met him, but his wife and daughters were ecstatic. They were no longer afraid of going out in public with him. His wife even related that kissing him was no longer an unbearable task. As they left, he turned his head slightly and gave me wink.

I saw him again for his regular maintenance that kept his condition in check. I am happy to have eliminated halitosis in the worst case I have ever seen.

MYTHS ABOUT HALITOSIS

A)   Halitosis comes from the stomach.

Not true. There are a series of valves in our stomachs and esophagus that block the regurgitation of our food. These valves also block any stomach odors from coming back up into the esophagus, our throats, and out our mouths or nose. Only in cases of certain illnesses can severe regurgitation occur.

Controlled gastroesophageal reflux disease does not exhibit this problem.

B) There is no cure for halitosis.

There is a **TOTAL CURE** that I will explain later. However, do not be misled by the companies that advertise a cure-in-a-bottle. What they offer is a temporary fix. **The TOTAL CURE does not depend on products to eliminate halitosis**.

C) If I brush or scrape my tongue, my bad breath will go away.

Scraping or brushing the tongue only removes **a thin, top layer** of a deep accumulation of bacteria, dead skin cells, dead blood cells, food, and debris which make up a major cause of the odor of bad breath.

D) Mouthwashes, mints, and gums can keep me halitosis free.

Companies that sell these products would like you to believe this; however, most products simply cover up the malodor with a stronger, more pleasant-smelling odor. This is true of every product that has a moderate-to-strong taste or odor. In addition, most contain some type of sugar that feed the bacteria, creating even more odor.

E) The foods I eat cause bad breath.

While it's true that onions and garlic, to mention just two foods, will taint your breath, they are not responsible for ongoing halitosis. They will, however, penetrate the coatings on the tongue and be absorbed into the bloodstream to be expelled in the breath from our lungs.

    F)   Better oral hygiene will solve my breath problem.

Better oral care will help overall, particularly when gingivitis or gum disease is present. However, halitosis is much more complex. So, establish good oral hygiene practices, and they will still serve you well, but not solve your breath problem.

    G)   Dipping my tongue scraper in special mouthwash will clean my tongue.

False. It is a sales technique for the mouthwash company. Will it help? Only a little, because a tongue scraper can only remove "yesterdays" coating, not what has piled up over the years and not the deeper coatings associated with chronic bad breath. Adding mouthwash does very little if anything. As you will see later, the coating, called a **biofilm** must be removed by means that are more sophisticated.

SIGNS & SYMPTOMS OF HALITOSIS

- Coating on tongue; coating can be white, yellowish, or brown
- People reacting to you in close situations; reactions like these are common:
    - Covering their nose or mouth
    - Stepping back or turning sideways
    - Offering you mints or gums
    - Rubbing under their noses
- Morning breath

- Brushing and flossing do little for the odor
- Regular mouthwashes wear off quickly
- Chronic bad taste that lasts more than 1 week
- Loss of some taste
- Food does not taste as profound
- Dry mouth
- Thick saliva
- Sinus problems & Allergies
- Post nasal drip

TEST YOURSELF FOR HALITOSIS

While many people with bad breath have tried the "lick the back of your hand" exercise, or the "cup your hands in front of your mouth" test, or even the "spoon" test, there is another test that involves your sight, your smell, and a piece of gauze. I routinely use it in my office in diagnosis and treatment.

Try this simple test to determine if you have a problem: Take a piece of sterile 2" x 2" gauze, available at every pharmacy. If you have a dry mouth, take 1 sip of water first and swish in your mouth for 30 seconds or so. Stick your tongue out as far as possible. To get the most coating, with your first two fingers on one side, and your thumb holding a corner on the other side, firmly wipe forward 3-4 times *from the farthest back* area that you can reach on your tongue. Get off as much coating as you can. Look at the gauze. Is it discolored? Compare the color to the white part of the gauze. Wait one minute. Smell the gauze. Is there an odor? If you see **either** a color on the gauze **or** smell an odor, you have halitosis.

One additional note: It is important when doing this test to wait a moment before smelling the gauze. Why? The same reason we have a hard time smelling our own bad breath— adaptation. However, even after waiting, *many people cannot smell their own odor on the gauze, because of this same phenomenon- adaptation.* You might want to include a close friend or relative to help with this test – someone who will tell you the truth without judgment.

Adaptation is a sensory phenomenon peculiar to taste and smell. Have you ever entered a room with a particularly bad odor or sat next to someone with a strong perfume? After a time, the odor seems to get better; the perfume seems to be more in the background. In reality, the odor is still there, but you have adapted to it and lost your awareness of it. So it is with halitosis. *It's also why our loved ones and even we may not notice it—they smelled it originally, but adapted to it as time went on.*

If you want to find out if others notice your breath, do not overlook the clues that they give you: A covered up nose when you are near someone, the intermittent rubbing and blocking of the nose, standing farther away than appropriate, turning sideways, and offering gums or mints may be indicators that you have a problem. Their actions should prompt you to find out if you do have bad breath by trying the tests above, asking a close friend, or by seeing a qualified professional.

In addition, trying to hide your bad breath with a strong but different odor is also a dead giveaway. Nothing screams "I have bad breath" than a strong minty odor. In addition, as that cover-up begins to dissipate, the actual odor of halitosis reemerges.

WHAT IS HALITOSIS?

Halitosis is a combination of odors that come from the waste products of various bacteria that live in our mouths and digest their "foods". These particular odors are usually Volatile Sulfur Compounds or VSCs for short, however, the same bacteria also produce other odor compounds that are not sulfur-based. The types of bacteria that produce VSCs are anaerobic bacteria, meaning they live without air. There are many places in the mouth that have little or no air: under the gums, in gum a disease areas, in food traps, in the coating on your tongue, in spaces between your teeth, and under poorly fitting fillings or crowns. Everywhere there is a dark, moist, air-deprived area in your mouth, you can be sure these anaerobic bacteria are breaking down their food, resulting in VSCs and other strong odor causing compounds that result in halitosis.

The bacterial "food" consists of proteins and sugars, dead mouth cells, dead blood cells, carbohydrates, and debris. Dead mouth cells accumulate as we slough off the mucous membrane lining of our mouths every day, like sloughing off the top-most skin cells on our bodies. In people with allergies or sinus issues, protein leaks onto the very back of the tongue, and, because of the bacteria, readily decomposes into Volatile Sulfur Compounds. Blood cells come from micro-bleeding occurring in the gums. Most people I see have not noticed any blood on their floss, toothbrush, or in the sink. Yet when I screen for bleeding, it is inevitably there, sometimes in many places. Removing the tongue coating and elimination of inflammation and bleeding of the gums is one cornerstone of our professional treatment.

As a point of interest, the anaerobic bacteria produce the following odor compounds:

ODOR COMPOUND	SMELL
Hydrogen Sulfide	Rotten Eggs
Methyl Mercaptan	Feces
Skatole	Mothballs
Cadavarine	Urine
Putrescine	Rotting Flesh
Isovaleric Acid	Sweat
Dimethyl Sulfide	Cabbage, Gasoline
Dimethyl Disulfide	Garlic

As you can see, there are a multitude of odor-causing compounds present in the breath. Only the ones outlined in grey are sulfur based. These are the only ones that are calibrated by the Halimeter to give a peak reading of sulfur compounds. The others are present to varying degrees and that is why we find that 80-90% of people have sulfur based compounds as the primary odor causing compound while the remaining people have more of a mixture that is not measured by the Halimeter. And, that is why there is no single test that measures the level of bad breath. At the National Breath Center we use four different tests to establish a diagnosis.

PART II

WHAT CAUSES BAD BREATH

THE CAUSES OF BAD BREATH

Research has shown that approximately 95% of halitosis comes from oral causes. Halitosis does *not* come from a "sour stomach," or ear, nose, and throat problems except in rare instances. As mentioned earlier, the actual odor of bad breath comes from the bacterial breakdown of its foods - proteins and sugars, dead mouth cells, dead blood cells, carbohydrates, and debris.

Based on over 22 years of personally treating and curing halitosis, I have identified 6 direct problems associated with bad breath:

1. Tongue biofilm coating (quantity & quality)
2. Bleeding gums, gingivitis, periodontal disease (severity)
3. Saliva and dry mouth
4. Food traps between the teeth
5. Other Factors :
    - Ill-fitting fillings, crowns, or bridgework
    - Missing teeth
    - Dentures, partials, and other appliances
    - Oral thrush and oral cancer
    - Other oral diseases
6. Sinus problems (see medical causes)

All of these create an environment for halitosis, causing bacteria to thrive, reproduce, and create more and more odor causing molecules.

When there is more than one factor, there is a multiplying effect. A tongue coating with bleeding gums enhances the bad breath exponentially, as do food traps, and other problems.

TONGUE ANATOMY

It is important to understand the anatomy of the tongue as the tongue biofilm coating is a primary, but not the only cause of halitosis.

The tongue is made up of four different papillae (projections) named filiform, fungiform, foliate, and circumvallate papillae, three of which are taste buds. The average number of individual taste buds on the tongue is about 9-10,000 with each taste bud having 50-150 cells which recognize taste.

The most important point to note about tongue anatomy is that every tongue is different. Some have fissures or grooves; some have denuded areas where there are no taste buds; and all people have taste buds of differing sizes, shapes, and depths. In fact, a condition known as geographic tongue actually changes the location of structures from time to time. Geographic tongue is *not* pathologic and is present in a small number of people.

All papillae have tiny arteries, veins, and nerves which connect to the major sensory nerve of the head that goes directly to the brain. Thus, taste is one of our senses that is near instantaneous.

The filiform papillae contain no taste buds but are the most numerous structures on the tongue. With some magnification, they look like blades of grass on a lawn; with higher magnification they are seen projecting off a base. The exact purpose of these papillae is not clear; however, they do act as a supporting structure for the actual taste buds and *especially accumulate the odor causing bacteria, volatile sulfur compounds, and other odor causing molecules.*

Fungiform papillae have taste buds as the primary part of their structure. They can taste salty foods, sour foods, bitter foods, and sweet foods. These papillae are shaped like a balloon with a wide base.

Foliate papillae lie in the posterior (back) areas of the tongue and are found on the borders of the tongue. They too are taste buds.

Circumvallate papillae are the fewest papillae on the tongue, and the largest of all. They are mushroom shaped and are in the back most part of the anatomical tongue. They number a maximum of 14 and are arranged in one V-like row separated by the middle of the tongue.

The sizes and shapes of our taste buds are what allow the bacteria and odors to get down to the *bottom of the tongue base, creating a biofilm, and what makes it so difficult to remove the total coating except by professional means.* These projections all accumulate bacteria, bacterial foods, and the odor-causing compounds. In people with bad breath, the taste buds are surrounded with **a thick, tenacious coating** that takes time to remove. However, once you are CURED, maintenance will hold the cure and keep bad breath from returning.

Behind the circumvallate papillae, where the tongue attaches to the throat, are finger-like projections referred to as the lingual tonsils that can be different sizes and shapes. They function as part of our immune system. Unfortunately, these projections also accumulate bacteria and VSCs like the rest of the tongue with the added disadvantage of accumulating sinus-related secretions like mucous, which is an excellent protein food for the odor-causing bacteria, especially with post-nasal drip.

TONGUE COATING

As mentioned earlier the tongue is the largest single structure for the accumulation of bacteria and their foods that cause mouth odor. The accumulation of dead skin cells, blood cells, debris, dead bacteria, sugars, carbohydrates, and other digestible bacterial matter is called the **biological film (biofilm)** or the tongue coating. Nothing can penetrate that thickness and adherence without mechanical removal. Even recent innovations like the sonic tongue cleaner cannot get down to the embedded layers. ***A biofilm can only be removed by mechanical action.*** In *Breath Odors,* the definitive professional book on halitosis, Nir Sterer and Mel Rosenberg, two premier researchers in the field of halitosis, state **"These oral biofilms are tissue-like structures consisting of cellular and extracellular matrix and are highly resistant to rinsing, washing, detergents, and even antibiotics. This is one reason why *mechanical cleaning procedures* - cleaning of dental and oral surfaces *are the cornerstone of oral hygiene"* (emphasis mine) *and the TOTAL CURE for halitosis.* Biofilms are living ecosystems.**

In professional treatment, we treat the tongue with a technique called Tongue Rejuvenation, which removes the biofilm; for the gums, the biofilm is removed by eliminating the tartar, smooth the outsides of the teeth where the biofilm is still attached, eliminate the inflammation and bleeding, and prevent it from reforming. It is important to note that most all tartar (calcium deposits with bacteria and debris) below the gums are small but have a big influence on bleeding and the dissolving of gum and bone. Finally, we teach each person how to do maintain themselves so that when they are cured they are less dependent on us.

The best analogy I have been able to think of for the tongue biofilm, is that of the front lawn of a house. The base of the tongue would be the dirt, while the lawn is made of grass, weeds, mushrooms, and the like. Everything above dirt level are the papillae and lingual tonsils packed together as one's lawn would be with small spaces between allowing insects (bacteria) to flourish. In our mouths, due to the thickness of layer upon layer of bacteria, their chemical waste (breath odor) that has been piling up for years or even decades, tongue scraping removes only the top layer while the biofilm (coating) keeps growing in the process, just like mowing the lawn removes only a top layer of what is growing there.

Why do some people with a tongue coating have chronic halitosis while some do not? It comes down to the anatomy of the tongue, the quantity and the quality of the biofilm itself, the virulence (activity) of the bacteria, oral hygiene practices, food traps, spaces between the teeth, and food and debris that add to the coating.

Coatings vary from person to person. Some coated tongues have low bacterial activity while others have high activity (halitosis sufferers). This leads to a difference in the quality of the biofilm. The quantity of the coating depends on the anatomy of the tongue. The more space there is between the taste buds, the more accumulation. And those who have no coating are the benefactors of low bacterial activity and an anatomy unfavorable to the accumulation of bacteria and their by-products.

Up to now, the only available treatment for the tongue coating has been tongue scraping. But tongue scraping only removes yesterday's layer. So, while the last bacteria and their waste products are removed, the vast majority of the biofilm remains. ***This is the key to CURING halitosis—removal of the biofilm down to the base of the tongue, complete removal of the biofilm under and between the teeth, and removal of the other factors that cause halitosis.***

BLEEDING, GINGIVITIS, & GUM DISEASE

Another primary concern, and a *direct cause of halitosis*, is the bacteria under the gums that are responsible for the early stages of gingivitis to the later stages of periodontal (gum) disease.

The anaerobic (without air) bacteria that cause halitosis are the ones that also cause gum disease and bleeding gums. In most cases, the gums become inflamed, a condition called gingivitis; in more advanced cases, bone loss accompanies the gum inflammation causing periodontal disease. As more biofilm accumulates, the deeper layers create a breeding ground for live bacteria. This makes removal of the bacteria-laden plaque under the gums even more difficult, and gum disease begins. As gum disease progresses, the gums pull away from the teeth, and the bone dissolves, creating gum pockets that allow more bacteria to accumulate at an even deeper level on the tooth root—a vicious cycle. Amazingly enough, this process is mostly painless!

The sulfur compounds from the bacteria actually damage the blood vessels in the gums and allow toxins into the body. It has been scientifically proven that these toxins in our bloodstream can directly affect our heart, brain, and other organs, sometimes leading to life-threatening diseases by increasing the inflammatory load on the body. Many other serious diseases are also the product of inflammation and can become worse from the toxins entering the blood vessels of the gums.

Perhaps you already know that one of the most important predictors of systemic disease is the inflammatory load on the body. When physicians measure C-reactive protein, they are measuring the amount of inflammation and thus the likelihood of serious disease occurring. And much of that can come from bacteria and toxins entering the tiny, broken blood vessels in the gums.

It's important to note that due to the lack of gum disease symptoms, bleeding, gingivitis, and periodontal disease must be assessed by a dentist. In our office, it is an important part of every initial and periodic examination. As a professional note, I see numerous people who have never had a gum exam or have had them sporadically. Because the potential for serious disease is very real, I would only see a dentist who performs a gum exam every year or sooner.

And, if you run into a dentist who says, "You're not bleeding too badly, don't worry about it," he or she is not the one you should allow to care for your teeth. Why? *Because it is in the early stages that gum disease can be cured! When cured, you no longer need worry about systemic inflammation coming from the gums.*

HOW DO *YOU* KNOW
THAT *YOU* HAVE GUM DISEASE?

Unfortunately, gum disease is usually silent, causing few noticeable symptoms. When it does cause symptoms, they are always painless, allowing many people to ignore the warning signs. *Because gum disease can occur with or without the presence of halitosis, I suggest you see a dentist who does a gum examination at least once per year.* Not even x-rays show gum disease in its early stages and sometimes in its moderate stage when it can be cured.

The principal signs of gum disease are:

- Bad taste or bad breath
- Slightly pink floss or toothbrush
- Floss that smells when you remove it from between your teeth
- Red, swollen, or tender gums
- Gums pulling away from the teeth
- A change in your bite

However, it is important to note that people cannot diagnose their own gum disease. The **only** way to determine if gum disease is present is to have a dentist perform a complete gum exam.

A gum examination requires measurements of the difference in gum attachment levels from the neck of the tooth to the height of the gum, with recordings of 6 different places around each tooth and notation of any site that bleeds. What should be looked for and recorded are all the places where there is bleeding and any place where the separation is greater than 3 millimeters.

SALIVA & DRY MOUTH

Saliva is our primary defense against oral disease. It plays a prominent role in bad breath in two ways. First, its acid level is important, and second, saliva carries oxygen, which neutralizes odors and bacteria to some degree.

The acidity or alkalinity of a substance is measured by its pH. The pH scale ranges between 0 and 14 with 7 being neutral; below 7 is acid and above 7 is alkaline. So, any acid level that gets farther from 7 and closer to 0 becomes more acidic, and an alkaline level that gets higher than 7 and closer to 14 becomes more alkaline. The closer to 7, the less acidic and the less alkaline. In anaerobic environments, these bacteria convert proteins and other sulfur compounds to H2S, hydrogen sulfide gas with a pH of 4.5, highly acid and **very** damaging.

The proper level of acidity or alkalinity in our bodies is essential for life. For instance, the correct acid-alkaline level for blood is 7.4. (Neutral is 7.0, making blood slightly alkaline.) Any large deviation from that, particularly for more than short periods of time, will cause severe disease, or disease can change the acid level of our blood and tissues. This is what the pH of hydrogen sulfide and the other odor-causing compounds do in the mouth.

The pH, or acid-alkaline level of our saliva varies from 6.2- to 7.4, straddling neutral but mostly acid. The pH of most areas of our bodies is not locked into one specific value but can handle deviations within a range. In a 1972 research paper, it was shown that normal saliva in the 6.5 range (slightly acidic), would cause no VSC odor, while at pH 7.5 an alkaline saliva makes halitosis possible and even severe, proving that moderately acidic saliva is inhibitory to malodor production (McNamara 1972). Of course, this means we want our saliva to be slightly acidic, not highly acidic like the hydrogen sulfide or even alkaline which promotes halitosis.

Here's how this relates to tongue coating and bacteria on the tongue. In an article published in the *Journal of Applied Oral Science*, the authors state that "salivary pH tended to be acidic while tongue coating pH tended to be alkaline." This means that there is a war going on between the saliva in our mouths and the tongue coating and its bacteria. In halitosis the coating and its bacterial content are winning. The more alkaline (above 7) the pH, the worse the halitosis.

Another beneficial property of saliva is that it carries oxygen. Oxygenation is a primary way to kill bacteria and neutralize the odors. Earlier I mentioned that the bacteria that cause bad breath are anaerobic (without air). Introducing oxygen into their environment will help the balance. This is called *buffering*. Unfortunately, once someone has halitosis, increasing oxygen in the solution is too little, too late and does not change the bacteria kill rate nor the odor elimination properties.

In the case of dry mouth, because the saliva volume is considerably less, there is little buffering, thus making the saliva less acidic and allowing the coating to dominate with greater numbers of bacteria, more odor, and little oxygenation. This problem, of course, leads to a stronger and more tenacious biofilm and a stronger halitosis. That's why I use saliva enhancing products in our office, for treatment at home, and in the Beating Bad Breath Protocol.

Dry mouth occurs from time to time in most of us when we are nervous or under stress. It has been shown by Queiroz in 2002 that stress can reduce saliva flow and cause an increase in VSCs. In 2006, Calil and Marcondes showed that anxiety also would elevate the VSCs.

However, some people do have a chronic dry mouth, which is called xerostomia and can stem from a medical condition or medications taken for certain problems. The list of drugs that cause dry mouth is long, some of which can be found in Appendix B.

Dry mouth is also a reason for "morning breath". When we sleep, our saliva flow stops. If we also sleep with our mouths open and breathe through our mouths, the air we inhale, along with the lessened saliva, dries the mouth lining further, allowing bacteria within the tongue coating, below the gums, and in the food trap areas to flourish and create even more of the same sulfur compounds that cause bad breath, resulting in worsened morning breath and a chronic halitosis.

Because morning breath *IS* halitosis, your breath should be tested to determine if chronic bad breath is a problem. And, if you are already using mouthwash, mints, or any product to freshen your mouth during the day, you already have chronic bad breath. It is easiest to cure at this stage than when one notices it during the day.

SPACES, FOOD TRAPS & OTHER PROBLEMS

Spaces between the teeth and the resulting **food traps** foster growth of bacteria and the odors they produce. It's not only that food gets between the teeth and ferments over time causing its own noxious odors, it is that a food trap is an opening where the odor-causing bacteria and the gum disease causes the bacteria to flourish. In food trap areas, the gums may bleed with normal brushing or flossing or be red and sore. These are indications of the bacteria causing damage to the gums (gum disease) through inflammation. The blood cells, dead skin, debris, mucous, and other bacterial by-products become primary food for the bacteria, the odors ensue, and gum disease progresses.

This is a much-overlooked cause as it requires a meticulous view of your mouth and a global look at bad breath. *If spaces exist between your teeth, or your dentist has not identified any of these situations, or recommended correcting them, see another dentist.*

Ill-fitting fillings, crowns, or bridges are other areas where the bacteria flourish and the odor abounds. By ill-fitting, I mean that the margins of the restoration near the edge of the filling, crown, or bridgework, especially near the gums, are not totally sealed.

Another way ill-fitting restorations occur is if they are not contoured properly on the back, front, and in between the teeth. You will know this if you get food trapped between or under them. *No restoration, filling, crown, implant, or bridge is acceptable* if it traps food. They may be ill-contoured at the outset or may become ill-contoured later, as the teeth drift or wear.

The problem for people is that ill-fitting dental work is usually not felt by the patient except sometimes as sensitivity, ledges that catch floss, or food traps. If you have any problems with recently done fillings or restorations, go back to your dentist. Do not wait because at a minimum it will cause gum inflammation and possible gum disease around the teeth.

If the restoration or filling is not done properly, the problem will manifest—it's only a matter of time. Only later, does a new cavity form, gum and bone loss ensue, or the restoration fails and needs redoing. That is why it is important to identify these problems early.

Dentures, partials, and dental appliances are another direct cause of mouth odor. The materials used to make almost all appliances are porous and absorb the odors of the mouth. And don't forget that your tongue can still have a long-standing coating where bacteria produce VSCs, which are absorbed into those materials over time. If you wear any of these appliances, I recommend using a Tru-**ACTIVE chlorine dioxide** mouthwash in a glass for about 5-10 minutes. If the appliance odor persists, increase your usage. Tru-ACTIVE chlorine dioxide not only kills the bacteria that cause the odor, but also the odor itself.

Missing teeth can also be a cause of bad breath. When teeth are removed and not replaced, the remaining teeth move up or down, backward or forward, but usually a combination of all *to close the gap*. That is the natural movement of teeth—to fill a space—and is a direct cause of exposed roots and spaces where food gets trapped. These areas will then have a different contour made for the accumulation of bacteria and mouth odor.

SINUS PROBLEMS & POST-NASAL DRIP

The bacteria that inhabit the sinuses are not the same type of bacteria that create VSCs in the mouth. However, in those with sinus problems, allergies, and post-nasal drip, there is an accumulation of mucous on the back part of the tongue and the lingual tonsils, which inhabit the area just behind where the tongue ends and the attachment to the pharyngeal wall (back of the throat) begins. This factor in bad breath must not be overlooked.

As the mucous drips onto the tongue and lingual tonsils, the anaerobic, halitosis-causing bacteria living there receive a rich source of food. The mucous contains proteins, primarily cysteine, which breaks down to hydrogen sulfide, and methionine, which breaks down to methyl mercaptans, thus creating even more VSCs. There are numerous people who take medications used to treat sinus problems and others that dry the mouth as a side-effect. Later I will talk about the best ways to eliminate this increase in VSCs and, generally to kill the bacteria and neutralize the odors on the back most part of the tongue, in the throat, and on the lingual tonsils, including the Most Effective Bacterial & Odor Killer.

If you have sinus problems, allergies, postnasal drip, and even asthma, consider a sinus irrigator described later. It is an all-natural way to relieve symptoms. If you are taking medication for these problems, they all are antihistamines or a similar drug that will dry the mouth. For halitosis, this must be treated with the proper dry mouth products, which I will outline later in this book.

NON-ORAL FACTORS IN HALITOSIS

Non-oral factors occur from outside the mouth or are brought into the mouth and can also cause or be contributors to bad breath.

Offending foods like garlic, onions, radishes, cabbage, cauliflower, and fermented foods change the breath. Bad breath from these foods starts when the membranes of our mouth and throat absorb some of these odors. The resulting odor can last a few hours or a few days.

When these foods are digested, small odor molecules get into our bloodstream, some finding their way to our lungs. Mixed with the air we breathe, we exhale these odor molecules, causing bad breath. For those with halitosis already, these foods complicate the odors and cause a more lasting effect.

Smoking is another non-oral cause of halitosis. The mixture of the chemicals in the smoke and the coating they create on the tongue make smokers non-curable unless they have given up the habit. If they have not, their best bet for improvement is the Beating Bad Breath Protocol© I will describe later. In my office we do not accept smokers as patients because the cure rate is zero.

Low carb diets, such as the Atkins diet, cause a direct change in body chemistry, sometimes creating mouth odor as a result. The reasons are two-fold. First, these diets cause a condition called ketosis in the body. Ketosis occurs when the body does not get enough carbohydrates, the primary fuel source for the body, and instead turns to fat stored in the body for energy, thus releasing ketone bodies. There are many of these, but a primary one that causes bad breath is acetone, which carries a fruity smell. Secondly, these diets contain an excess of protein, some of which are broken down to ammonia, another odor-causing chemical. These odors are commonly called "keto-breath." So while you may lose weight on diets such as this, be aware that long-term dieting this way may directly cause chronic bad breath.

WHAT SHOULD YOU EAT WITH HALITOSIS?

The goal is to eat the foods that combat bacteria and help moderate the coating on the tongue. This starts with fresh fruits and vegetables for two reasons: first, the chewing action will help rub off some of the coating on the tongue, and second it will also help create more saliva, the benefits of which I mentioned earlier. Raw vegetables are one of the best foods to eat because of their cleansing action when chewing, not to mention their nutritional value.

WHAT YOU SHOULD NOT EAT WITH HALITOSIS

While *occasional* foods like onions or garlic will add to your breath problem, you should avoid any type of food that directly adds to the biofilm coating. Dairy products are at the head of the list. This includes milk, cheese, yogurt, ice cream—in fact, anything that coats the tongue. Remember the test for halitosis? Try it after you drink a glass of milk or have some cheese. You will smell the milky sour smell of bad breath that has now become the top layer of your tongue coating.

Broccoli, cauliflower, and radishes are in a class by themselves. They are beneficial to the tongue coating and cleansing, but in some people, leave behind a strong odor. If you eat these foods raw, I would personally test them before a social occasion to determine if they help or hurt our breath. To test them, eat them for dinner and ask a loved one to give you their opinion.

Other foods that coat the tongue are coffee and tea, adding to the thickness of the coating while mixing noxious components and worsening the problem.

PART III

MEDICINE & HALITOSIS

MEDICAL CAUSES OF HALITOSIS

While halitosis is overwhelmingly (95%) caused by problems in the mouth, there are some medical problems that are important to explore. Listing them all in this book would be of little use because almost every one is a disease with symptoms far worse than halitosis and for which one would have surely sought medical help. However, I will focus on a few that may cause a breath issue and are the most relevant in halitosis.

We've already mentioned sinus problems, allergies, and post-nasal drip as contributors to halitosis; any illness involving the lungs, like bronchitis or pneumonia, can cause bad breath until it is under control or eliminated. The same can occur with illnesses involving the pharynx, to which the tongue attaches. The pharynx is that area behind and below the anatomical tongue yet above the esophagus. A bad case of pharyngitis can create noxious odors, but again, the other symptoms would have led you to your physician. The big concern in all odors that are extremely fetid and do not subside is cancer. Cancer can leave large and small internal, unhealed sores that will cause odors.

Other possible contributors can be a hiatal hernia or gastroesophageal reflux disease (GERD) yet both are uncommon. I say contributors as these *may* allow *some* odors into the mouth as the lower esophageal valve, one of the valves that seal the stomach, may be ill functioning and allow some food to be retained in the esophagus. But unless the cases are extreme, their effect should be negligible. Again, since their nature is more serious than bad breath, most people would have already seen their doctor and been treated.

Diabetes Type I or II are of particular concern. Their odors are a sweet, fruity, acetone-like odor; however, as long as diabetes is controlled, there is no cause for the bad-breath alarm. One important note about diabetes: because diabetes makes people more prone to infection, the fragile blood vessels of gum disease are a particular problem among diabetics. And with the bleeding of the gums, not only do we need to be concerned about infection, but also the multiplication of a primary bacterial food (dead blood cells) that cause halitosis and gum disease. If you are diabetic, see your dentist regularly for dental cleanings and yearly gum measurements. An examination that shows gum disease must be treated, not just because of halitosis, but because of the systemic implications. Moreover, see your physician to monitor your problem.

One problem that contributes to bad breath is tonsil stones, medically called tonsilloliths, which are not really stone-like but mushy white accumulations in the palatine tonsils at the back of the throat. When present, they accumulate bacteria and partially digested food and create odors (VSCs), which can be quite profound. If you have one, your dentist should be able to remove it. And be sure to follow-up yourself with **ACTIVE** chlorine dioxide rinses.

MEDICATIONS CONTRIBUTE TO HALITOSIS

The list includes antihistamines and antidepressants, but since it is long, I have included only some of these medications in the Appendix. I believe it is more important to understand what these have in common that causes them to contribute to halitosis: they greatly reduce the amount of saliva and dry the mouth, sometimes severely.

At the National Breath Center, I always review everyone's health history, illnesses, and medications and talk to each person about them. However, medications are a fact of life, so rather than attempt to manage salivation for different medications, any treatment plan should always include a saliva enhancer and a recommendation to drink 6-8 glasses of water each day. These are the least expensive and easiest ways to create more saliva that can then help buffer the tongue coating and wash away more bacteria for anyone who has bad breath.

THE PSYCHOLOGY OF HALITOSIS

Despite the article in the *Journal of Breath Research,* "Breaking Paradigms: A New Definition for Halitosis in the Context of Pseudo-halitosis and Halitophobia" which states "It is known that almost one-third of patients who seek treatment for bad breath do not have genuine halitosis", this is *not* what I have seen in my practice. In the 22+ years I have been treating and curing bad breath, only a small number of people did not have noticeable bad breath.

However, there are two psychological conditions that are relevant here: halitophobia and Olfactory Reference Syndrome. The latter is where the person is preoccupied that their body odor is always there and always offensive even when there is no odor. The key word here is preoccupied. Those that are preoccupied with mouth odor when they do not have bad breath at all are said to have halitophobia, or delusional halitosis. While I am not a researcher, I am a clinician who has seen these types of problems. They are diagnosed by measuring the breath of a person with a complaint of chronic halitosis but finding no positive test results.

The other type of halitophobia is impossible to detect at the outset. In these people, their halitophobia manifests after they have been objectively cured but still insist that they notice reactions to their breath. Since they must pass the 4 tests we originally give for halitosis before we pronounce a CURE, I know that these people have a psychological problem around their breath problem which no longer exists.

THE BAD BREATH BRUSH-OFF

After over 22 years of observation and listening, here is my understanding of the ways our minds work in regard to bad breath.

The first item to note is that many of the people I see are the ones who have tried every product, seen multiple dentists, perhaps seen some physicians, and even visited a breath clinic or dentist who claims they "specialize" in bad breath. These are the people "without hope" as they put it.

They have experienced the Bad Breath Brush-Off in many ways and over much time. This has led to feelings of hopelessness, despair, and fear of rejection. Hopelessness, as they have found nothing that works; despair that they ever will; and fear of social rejection and never living a normal life. They would not feel this way unless they had bad breath and had experienced the bad breath brush-off. It is the reaction of others that has caused this eruption of emotional issues and the lack of knowledge of the dental profession about what causes bad breath.

When others brace themselves from your breath, you feel rejected. Stepping back, offering mints, and covering noses creates an expectation that others will always do that and that you will always have bad breath. For the person doing that behavior, it is another manifestation of adaptation, a normal phenomenon. They are adapting to protect themselves from odor. In essence, *each party is reacting to each other's actions*.

For the people who interact with someone with halitosis, they have usually done it so often that it is like a reflex— automatic because of their ingrained expectation of a definitive, unpleasant odor that has been there for some time. Of course, when someone is cured, these people do not know it, so they may continue to react the same way for a time.

While this transition can be difficult for both sides, the testing we do at the end of the treatment and any time thereafter plus the testing people can do on their own proves they have no discernible breath odor. In many people, this alone raises the confidence level of these former halitosis sufferers.

Here's the story of a couple who almost didn't get together because of the Bad Breath Brush-Off as told to me by my patients' girlfriend when she came with him for his first maintenance visit 6 months later.

Mark & Susan

When our date was over, Mark walked me up the stairs to my apartment. The evening was near ending and I could tell Mark was beginning to feel a bit nervous. I didn't know it at the time, but he was worried I wouldn't kiss him goodnight.
We had had a very nice evening, finding that we had a lot in common and were deep in conversation at the restaurant until after 1 AM.
"Thanks for a nice evening, Mark", I said.
"I had a good time too. May I kiss you goodnight?"
Smiling, I nodded my approval.
As Mark got close, I had a reflexive action. The instant I detected his breath, I turned my head and his kiss landed on my cheek. Mark turned and ran down the stairs.
I found out later that Mark was devastated by my reaction. We had known each other for six months before he got up the courage to ask me out. And now, after that first date which had gone so well until the end, I doubted I'd see him again.
But Mark was really intent on not having our first date be our last, so he decided to find out why. The next morning, he took a piece of gauze from his medicine chest and wiped his tongue. It was yellow, he later told me. Then he smelled the gauze and found a strong odor.
As he told me, he asked Rick, his best friend to confirm whether he had bad breath. So he asked him.
Rick confirmed it and referred Mark to you.
He told me he waited to be sure his bad breath was gone, and after you cured his problem, he celebrated by sending me a dozen roses with this note:
"Problem solved. How about Saturday night?"

Then I noticed the ring on her finger.

PART IV

CURRENT TREATMENT

RESEARCH

What does dentistry currently know about the clinical treatment of halitosis? I am sorry to say, but virtually nothing that will cure halitosis. While I have been curing bad breath for decades and presented my technique to over 10,000 dentists, I can no longer find a dentist that does actual treatment anymore; they seem to rely on the sales of products.

In adding my notes from the 60 previous years of research that I studied in the 1990s and studying the research about halitosis for the last 20 years, I found no awareness of the real cure for halitosis.

Recently there has been great interest in altering the oral bacteria and replacing the "bad" bacteria with non-pathogenic bacteria produced by probiotics. One of those papers is "Effects of Chewing Gum Containing the Probiotic Bacterium *Lactobacillus Reuteri* to Oral Malodor." The researchers concluded that while the organoleptic (smell) scores were lower, "assessments of the VSC levels displayed no significant differences." While there is merit in all research, even those looking for the "right" bacteria to counteract the odor-causing ones, their direction does not acknowledge where the real problems lie.

More recent research has identified one strain of bacteria, *S.Salivarius* K-12 that displaces the pathogenic bacteria of bad breath to some degree. Unfortunately, it comes as a lozenge and even when sucked on, cannot get to the deeper layers of the biofilm.

The TOTAL CURE restores the balance of bacteria by removing the bad bacteria, their "foods", and the debris so the beneficial bacteria can emerge in greater numbers and activity.

While many studies around the world each year regard one or another aspect of halitosis, I believe that the researchers are looking in the wrong place. The cure is literally right under their noses.

THE FUTURE

While it is possible that a magic pill or liquid will be invented to cure halitosis, it is highly unlikely. Why? The same reason the cure-in-a-bottle internet products don't cure people – they cannot reach the middle and deepest layers of the biofilm.

However, there is an exciting development that I want to tell you about that will be available in the summer of 2015 –the Breathometer Mint. As a leading expert in curing bad breath, I have helped develop this pocket size instrument that actually measures the VSCs in your breath and displays them on your smartphone. There will be no more need to lick your hand, cup your hands or even smell the gauze to determine the level of bad breath you have. I am so excited about this product that I have accepted the position of Dental Director at this company and, I plan to give one of these instruments to each of my patients to measure their breath between visits.

So, if you are looking for a way to determine how much of a breath problem you have, pick up a Breathometer Mint when they become available. And tune into our website for an accurate calibration of the Mint and all the latest information about its development and use.

THE AMERICAN DENTAL ASSOCIATION

When I wrote the previous edition of this book in 2013, on the ADA's web page regarding halitosis, you were greeted by the following statement:

"There is no professional/clinical information on this topic."

I am happy to say that they now reference some studies on bad breath as totally inadequate as it is.

GOOGLE SEARCH

The downside of an internet search is that it also includes eBooks, home remedies created or recommended by so-called "experts" who have found the "magic formula" that will cure you too. Some even relate personal experiences that they say will apply to you, many to the tune of $39.95 for their secret.

Having seen over 7,000 people since my treatment and subsequent cure began, I am sorry to say that no such remedy exists. While many compounds or techniques can affect mouth odor temporarily, they always fail. My patients can attest to that.

In an attempt to determine the state of halitosis in industry, dental offices, breath clinics and information about products and other treatments, I conducted a lengthy Google search. It is not possible to list all that I learned; however, I am listing the top eight results for the term "bad breath" at the time of the search, April 2015.

The first unpaid search item was from Web MD, titled "Dental Health and Bad Breath" which had the usual basic information. It was slanted toward a medical point of view spending too much space on medical possibilities, without even mentioning biofilms. Their recommendations are so basic they are not worth mentioning as they will make no difference in someone with bad breath.

The second result leads to the most heavily advertised products on the internet – Therabreath. It must be noted that, even though they advertise their products as active chlorine dioxide, it is not. Therabreath is stabilized sodium chlorite, a less strong bacterial killer and odor neutralizer than active ClO2.

The third result in the unpaid search list was Wikipedia. Not surprisingly, it had the most pertinent and voluminous information on halitosis. If I were personally looking for answers, I'd start there. However, at the time of this writing, Wikipedia had a medical perspective that I have found has little impact in bad breath. In addition, as I stated earlier, I have not seen that 25% of people seeking professional help have halitophobia, as noted earlier.

The fourth entry comes from mercola.com, a natural health proponent who puts out a newsletter and sells a lot of products that he mentions in his newsletters. Hardly an objective guide. However, he does mention some of the mouthwash treatments available and a large paragraph on dry mouth. To end the section on bad breath, he talks about the bacteria in our gut, which while important, has little to do with oral bacteria. The same strains in the mouth are not found in the gut due to the different acid levels.

The next listed search result under bad breath is titled simply "Bad Breath" from the Mayo clinic. You would expect a trove of essential information from Mayo, but it only contains 5 worthless paragraphs. This makes it easy to see why physicians do not consider bad breath a problem.

The fifth search result was titled "Halitosis Causes and Halitosis Information" and located at another product selling site.

The sixth search result is from the Mayo Clinic, "Bad Breath – mayoclinic.com." Like many sites, it takes the same basic information and rewrites it; however, this site offers more information from the dental side where the problem originates.

The seventh search result comes from emedicinehealth.com which had the usual information; however, it was written by two physicians. I find it difficult to rate this information as definitively helpful when written by physicians who most likely see only people with bad breath caused by serious illnesses. Physicians are not experts on bad breath, no matter their field.

The last search result in the top eight is the American Dental Association entry. This link is woefully inadequate in all categories of information. Under causes of bad breath they only list: food, gum disease, dry mouth, smoking, and medical conditions. It is no wonder that insurance companies do not pay for a bad breath cure when the ADA hardly recognizes it as a problem.

So what does this list and the others I followed from Google tell me? Two things. First, people are looking for the best information about bad breath they can find; and second, there is little if any information about the CURE that has existed for over 22 years.

WHY OVER-THE-COUNTER BREATH PRODUCTS DO NOT WORK

Contrary to millions of dollars of advertising and 95% of all oral care shelf space in the pharmacy, over-the-counter (OTC) products are almost totally ineffective for breath problems and gum disease - no matter what the advertising label says about germ killers.

A primary reason OTC products do not work is that they dry out the mouth tissues. In addition, OTC products that claim to help bad breath simply lay a more pleasant odor over the layer of bad breath odor that exists at that time. It is the strength of the chemicals that influences the time it lasts, as that more pleasant odor is being overpowered by the odor of bad breath that exists directly beneath it.

Why do breath products not work? Here are three other reasons:

- They do not kill the bacteria that cause halitosis or neutralize the odors of bad breath; in other words, they may be disinfectants good for wiping down surfaces, but the bacteria they target are not specific for oral bacteria, despite the astringent feeling

- The acid level does not match the saliva level.
  - o Acid levels must be balanced—not too acid, not too alkaline. (Remember that saliva is pH 6.2 to 7.4.)
- They use chemicals like phenol and essential oils like menthol that strongly dry the mouth.
  - o Dry mouth is a major cause of halitosis.

A complex set of ingredients goes into mouthwash products. It has been my experience that due to their mouth-drying effects, lack of significant bacterial kill, and the use of strong odors to cover up bad breath, I have not recommended these products since the early 1990s.

DOES FRESH BREATH REALLY EXIST?

Yes, but not as you would imagine. Here's why. The opposite of bad breath is not fresh breath, which connotes the odor of something fresh-smelling like mint, flowers, fabric softener, hair shampoo, or soap.

The true opposite of bad breath is no discernible breath. In other words, your breath is not noticeable. No one can smell it.

From my research, it appears that "fresh breath" came into vogue in the roaring 1920s, right after the Great War (WWI) when the world was feeling prosperous and ready to embrace new ideas. It was a time of great optimism as vast new possibilities were open: electricity available to almost everyone, affordable cars and luxury ones, and travel as entertainment. At this time too, hospitals, pharmaceutical companies, and doctors all flourished with new techniques and drugs to try and profits to be had.

It was during this time that the practice of sterilization flourished. The idea of killing bacteria was now in vogue.

With this as background, Listerine mounted an advertising campaign that pronounced Listerine as the cure for chronic halitosis. The public readily agreed, especially because the formulation, with 26% alcohol, which is now believed toxic by many, created a noticeable astringency that caused people to believe their mouth was being sterilized. Listerine became the best-selling mouthwash for decades, and the idea of fresh breath, now defined by astringency and a strong odor, took off.

Yes. I know. Thanks to Madison Avenue, we all believe that fresh breath has a "fresh" smell, usually minty. *However, breath that is not noticeable is the only true fresh breath. Because **true fresh breath is the absence of odor**.* Who wants anyone to notice their breath? There is literally *no discernible odor* in fresh breath.

The goal of halitosis treatment and the TOTAL CURE is to eliminate the bacteria and the odor-causing compounds to create NO ODOR.

(In the following text, some terms are used that need clarification. Chlorine dioxide is a compound whose chemical abbreviation is as follows: ClO2. ClO2 represents the elements used in the compound. Capital "C" and small "l" are for chlorine; capital "O" is for oxygen; and the "2" represents 2 elements of oxygen in its molecular form. This chemical abbreviation is pronounced: C L Oh 2. True ACTIVE

chlorine dioxide is a superior bacterial and odor killer that is NON-TOXIC to any oral tissue and by its mechanism DOES NOT create any bacterial immunity)*

THE IDEAL MOUTHWASH & TOOTHPASTE

Now that we have covered the dubious effectiveness of OTC products and some of their undesirable side effects, *I want to detail an **ideal** breath odor product AND a superior oral care product.* After using and testing products for over 20 years, I had become discouraged. Personally and professionally, using scientific instruments and other tests I use at the **National Breath Center**, I had never found a product that meets all the following requirements. This has been my wish list and why I decided to collaborate with a manufacturer and offer the **SUPREME BREATH™ Tru-ACTIVE Mouthwash and Toothpaste.** *They are what I give to my patients and what I and my family use.*

*Why did I help develop Supreme Breath™ Tru-ACTIVE chlorine dioxide (ClO2)?? **Because it satisfies all the criteria below and THEY WORK! After going through dozens of products with many claims, I decided to help develop one that truly works.***

Here is what I recommend to everyone in a breath product and oral care product:

1) **A product that almost instantly eliminates bacteria and that does not cause bacterial resistance**

   Since anaerobic (without air) bacteria are the ultimate culprits in halitosis, the perfect product must kill them near instantly. This is where **Tru-ACTIVE chlorine dioxide (ClO2)** products come in. These are the products of choice because they have a 100% kill rate in minutes. But also important is the means of action. They must ONLY destroy bacteria, not mouth tissue.

2) A product that eliminates odor immediately

As we have seen, OTC products do nothing to neutralize the odors of bad breath. The perfect mouthrinse must eliminate these odor molecules almost instantly. Rinsing, which distributes the solutions throughout the mouth, must result in near instant elimination of odor molecules as well as the highest bacterial kill rate achievable. That is why rinsing and gargling is so important: it also cleans the backmost part of the tongue where a disproportionate number of the odor molecules and these bacteria live.

3) A product that kills the bacteria that cause gum disease

Tru-ACTIVE ClO2 kills anaerobic bacteria (without air) that cause and perpetuate gum disease —When rinsing or being delivered into the gum areas with an oral irrigator, the anti-bacterial action is directed down into the gum pockets where the bacteria live and flourish, and are killed near instantly.

4) A product that allows YOU to control its strength

Tru- ACTIVE ClO2, can be mixed as needed allowing you to control the strength. In the Beating Bad Breath

Protocol detailed later, you want one strength that you can vary the mix for the severity of bad breath; for the gauze protocol you need another strength; and for use in the oral irrigator you want a different strength. In the *Beating Bad Breath Protocol©* I detail the uses for different strengths and how to vary the strength.
This property - mixing when needed and the ability to vary strength - allows each person to have TOTAL control over the product they use.

Varying the strength is a very important property. Not only does it allow YOU to customize your treatment and results, but when new techniques or instruments come along, you will be able to adapt the product to the technique and not be stuck with only one strength.

5) A product that does no harm

Alcohol-based products dry your mouth, may cause oral cancer with long-term use, and are not to be swallowed. I recommend rinsing and gargling with **Tru-ACTIVE ClO2** mouthrinse to not only kill the bacteria that cause halitosis and gum disease, but to kill the odor as well. I also recommend it to kill throat bacteria and kill the odor within the lingual tonsils at the back of the tongue where the tissue is much softer. This is also especially helpful for sinus drainage. **Tru-ACTIVE ClO2** products do not cause dry mouth nor create any of the other problems that OTC products do.

6) A product that works and that you can depend on

In 1995, I wrote the first book on halitosis, *Beating Bad Breath*. While two of three experts at the time chose to produce and sell products, I chose the path that would get the correct treatment to as many people as possible - treating people at the National Breath Center and teaching dentists how to cure bad breath themselves. I had hoped that more dentists would help more people cure their life-altering condition as I was. But it was not to be. Thus, for a time I used the products of others as part of my TOTAL CURE protocol.

That gave me an advantage that few have – the ability to see just what works and what doesn't. And to watch for success OR vary the treatment to accommodate an individual's own unique situation.

After testing the available chlorine dioxide products personally and with patients, I observed that they did not fit the above criteria nor were they doing the job that I needed for the TOTAL CURE. That is why **SUPREME BREATH™ Tru-ACTIVE Chlorine Dioxide (ClO2)** exists. Later I will discuss the differences between "stabilized chlorine dioxide" (not even chlorine dioxide) and SUPREME BREATH™ Tru-ACTIVE chlorine dioxide.

I would not offer this product if I had not personally tested it and if I did not believe it is the BEST available. I use it for maintenance of the TOTAL CURE to help keep the tongue biofilm (coating) from returning. I also recommend it to all periodontal disease patients as I have seen it do a better job than anything else on the market. And, as the most effective product I have ever used, it is a part of the Maintenance Protocol and the Beating Bad Breath Protocol for those who choose the self-help route.

INEFFECTIVE CURRENT PROFESSIONAL TREATMENT

Walk into a fresh breath clinic or a dentist who says they treat bad breath, and you'll most likely walk out with your teeth cleaned and a basketful of products. That's the current professional treatment for halitosis. ***Eliminating the causes simply does not exist.***

The resident blogger on bad breath from the Dr. Oz show says you can take control of your breath in this way:

- "Have your teeth professionally cleaned at least three times a year.
- Floss every day.
- Brush at least twice a day.
- Brush and scrape your tongue frequently.
- Try an antibacterial gel.
- Use an alcohol-free mouthwash once a day.
- Use antibacterial sprays. They're also a quick way to give your mouth a clean sweep. Stick one in your purse or leave it by the front door so you'll get into the habit of using it right before you leave the house.
- Drink water frequently, both to keep lingering food particles from sticking, as well as to fend off dry mouth.
- Eat right. Choose less acidic food and balance the pH levels in your mouth."

The sum total of all these, while helpful, will essentially get you nowhere if you have halitosis. That's the state of knowledge for current dentists.

A "top dentist" in halitosis diagnosis and treatment, as he says on his website with the logos of some of the television programs he has been on, *does no treatment whatsoever*. His protocol is only an initial consultation and limited diagnosis; his treatment is a basketful of products. Even more, his nurse tells people who call that if they come from out of town, they may not even need a follow-up visit because they will most likely be cured after the first visit—*a claim with no actual treatment*. One size fits all.

As I will detail in a following chapter, hands-on treatment is the gold standard that most every dentist fails to follow. It is the only way to expertly treat and CURE people that works.

In the meantime, beware of people who offer a cure with no real treatment behind it. And beware of internet cures-in-a-bottle. Later I will give you a list of questions to ask an office that advertises that they treat bad breath to determine if they actually do use the proper techniques.

That brings us to the definition of a CURE.

A CURE should eliminate the problem itself, all related causes, and provide the means to keep halitosis from coming back.

This definition is important because it excludes anything that needs to be used every day like over-the

counter- mouthwashes and internet cures – in – a - bottle. More importantly it defines professional treatment necessary to achieve a Total Cure.

PART V

THE SOCIAL DILEMMA

Perhaps you didn't just pick this book for yourself. Perhaps your real motivation is the bad breath of a friend, a business associate, or a loved one. Now that you know how to determine if *you* have bad breath, how do you tell someone close to you?

The truth is that no matter how you do it, it is difficult. You don't want to hurt someone's feelings, and they may feel they are being singled out or that people know their secret. But keep one thing in mind. Halitosis is caused by bacteria that also cause periodontal disease, which causes people to lose teeth. And the bleeding of gingivitis or gum disease increases the overall inflammation in someone's body, an inflammation that is a marker for far more serious problems. It is not just an odor. And, there is a cure that others may not know about. So, you are really doing someone a great service by giving them information that affects their health. You only need to find the best way to communicate it for you both.

How you tell someone that he or she has halitosis will depend on a variety of factors. To begin with, ask yourself:

- How well do you know this person?
- What is your relationship?
- How can I tell them without offending?
- When would be the best time? The best place?

The approach you use depends on the relationship you have with this person. While this chapter will offer you a number of suggestions, only you can determine the best way to approach the subject of bad breath.

Here's how Tom did it before his wife became a patient of mine.

The interview was only 2 weeks away, and Tom was getting nervous for his wife—she had bad breath. Mary was applying for a new job and wanted everything to be perfect. She had purchased a new suit and was to have her hair done next week. But as optimistic as she was, Tom had some concerns about her breath, especially since she had not had her teeth cleaned in three years.

Tom took responsibility and asked, "Honey, have you noticed that your breath is off?" While Tom had known for some time, it only recently had reached the point where he could smell it before he got close. Perhaps the interviewer would do the same.

"Tom, I didn't know about my breath, but I have had a bad taste for some time, and it seems to be getting worse. I do not know if I have a problem or not. And with that interview coming up I am beginning to worry - a lot."

So Tom took the matter in his own hands and searched the Internet for a dentist who could help. Tom interviewed some of the office staff when he called to find out exactly what the dentist did and became discouraged after a couple of hours of phone calls. Then he called me.

Tom had discovered that I had written the book Beating Bad Breath *and explained the circumstances of his wife's problem. With less than two weeks away, I offered him two alternatives: first, to try the Beating Bad Breath Protocol I had been using for patients, and second, to come and see me.*

Tom and Mary elected to do both and set up an appointment for that Thursday. Upon examination it was easy to tell that Mary had a problem that had become severe. I volunteered to come into the office every day for the next four days to help her. She agreed to start the protocol immediately.

Her breath was within normal limits a few days before her interview.

Two weeks later, I received a nice thank you card that read,

Dr. Miller,

I could not have done it without you. I got the job and I am very excited!
Thanks,
Mary

Tom and Mary were close in their relationship, and Tom knew that if said in a way that would not offend her, Mary would act on the information.

Perhaps you know someone you are close to who would appreciate the news the way Tom told Mary.

Here are some other suggestions:

1. To begin, it's important to be as gentle and sincere as possible. In discussing this problem with someone you care about, think about the words you would use to describe their bad breath. It would be wise to use words like "off," "sour," or "noticeable" rather than "offensive" or "pungent."

2. Approach the person with a question, not a statement. Instead of telling them that they have a problem, start by asking if they have noticed any change in their breath or taste. Whatever they reply, just tell them you are concerned because you've noticed something.

3. You might want to try an optimistic approach: "You know Sam, there's something I've been thinking about telling you for some time. But until now, I didn't have any good suggestions. Now, I do. This book may be just the thing."

The key to having a meaningful discussion without hurting someone's feelings is to create that conversation in a safe place, away from other colleagues, and in an environment that is calming. If you do this, and speak from the heart, people may be taken aback that others know about their breath (they think they have been successful covering it up) but will appreciate your sincerity. That's the best way to help others – kindness, sincerity, and caring.

PART VI

THE PROFESSIONAL APPROACH

THE TOTAL CURE

Despite selling products on the internet with advertised "99.7%" cures, *there is a **REAL CURE**—*the one I have been using for 22 years, **and the *only one that does not need repeating nor relies on products to eliminate bad breath*.**

Remember the six areas where halitosis comes from?

Biofilm coating on the tongue and under the gums (quantity & quality)

Bleeding gums, gingivitis, periodontal disease (severity and number of areas)

Saliva and dry mouth

Food traps between the teeth; open contacts

Sinus problems

Other Dental Factors:

- Ill-fitting fillings, crowns, or bridgework
- Missing teeth
- Dentures, partials, and other appliances
- Oral thrush and oral cancer
- Other oral diseases

Because many of these issues are usually present, a comprehensive professional approach is needed to CURE halitosis and prevent its return.

To keep you from waiting any longer, the largest parts of the TOTAL CURE are these: total removal of the biofilm (coating) on the tongue; elimination of bleeding gums and any gum disease; increased saliva production; and elimination of food and bacterial traps. I call them, "The Big 4".These problems are all treated in Phase 1 of our TOTAL CURE program.

BIOFILMS

As mentioned earlier, biofilms form where bacteria and debris come together. Thus, there are biofilms on the tongue and biofilms around the teeth.

This bears repeating: In *Breath Odors, a professional book by* Nir Sterer and Mel Rosenberg, they state, "**These oral biofilms are tissue-like structures consisting of cellular and extracellular matrix and are highly resistant to rinsing, washing, detergents, and even antibiotics. This is one reason why *mechanical cleaning procedures* - cleaning of dental and oral surfaces *are the cornerstone of oral hygiene.*"** (emphasis mine)

Biofilms are living ecosystems and can only be removed by mechanical means.

It is also the cornerstone of the TOTAL CURE for bad breath. Biofilm removal on the tongue, under the gums, and between the teeth is the KEY to eliminating halitosis. At the National Breath Center the tongue treatment is called Tongue Rejuvenation.

Tongue Rejuvenation (patent pending) removes the entire tongue biofilm all the way down to the base of the tongue. As this happens, the bacteria are eliminated, the odors removed, and the tongue becomes healthy again. No odor, no bacteria, no biofilm,

THE BIG FOUR

1. TONGUE BIOFILM REMOVAL

If you remember the earlier description of the taste buds that make up the majority of surface area on our tongues, and that an individual's tongue anatomy determines the size, depth, quality, and tenaciousness of its biofilm, you probably know that not only have these coatings been piling on microscopic layer by layer over years or even decades, their removal can take time.

Using Tongue Rejuvenation, a proprietary technique that is painless and highly effective, we can return someone's tongue to health—no coating, no discernible odor measured by the Halimeter, the two gauze tests, or the organoleptic test - the same 4 tests we use at the initial diagnosis described later we can create 100% success with no discernible bad breath. And it can be maintained by everyone! See some before and after photos on our website www.beathalitosis.com.

2. BLEEDING GUMS

Very little emphasis has been made in the clinician's office that emphasizes bleeding over outright gum disease. Certainly, studies have been done that show halitosis gets better when any kind of gum disease is treated. However, our goal is the elimination of the bacteria that causes the bleeding and gum disease. While inside the tiny blood vessels in the gums themselves, the blood cells are alive; once minor inflammation occurs, these tiny blood vessels break and let these blood cells out, which immediately die and serve as food for the gum disease causing bacteria. It is the bleeding that is important in halitosis and is also part of the vicious cycle of gum disease. Thus, our cure must also treat the bleeding areas and help each person eliminate them from their own mouths.

In addition, our treatment of gum disease can also serve as an alternative to painful gum surgery in most cases.

3. DRY MOUTH & SALIVA ENHANCEMENT

We have previously discussed dry mouth and its importance in bad breath. It is an important factor for many people in eliminating bad breath. At the National Breath Center, we recommend different over-the-counter remedies depending on someone's situation. One that we recommend is the Ora-Moist dry mouth patch to wear during the day and night. It does not interfere with any other part of the protocol but is a big help for everyone, even if one does not have a noticeable saliva deficiency. Other saliva enhancers include Xylitol gums and lozenges, Xylimelt wafers, and sipping from a water bottle all day long. Be sure to check the ingredients of anything you use so that they do not contain any artificial sweeteners to enhance the flavor or anything artificial like colors or fillers.

Remember, the more saliva there is to wash away bacteria and the odors, the less prominent the breath problem.

4. SPACES, FOOD TRAPS, AND OTHER DENTAL CONDITIONS

Think of it this way: When food gets trapped between the teeth, the immediate reaction of the body, from bacteria that are covered up and protected by the food and debris packed on top, is inflammation, which as I've mentioned leads to bleeding that feeds the bacteria. So, if not corrected, there is a constant supply of dead blood cells, odor-causing bacteria, and fermented food that never leaves. Multiply this by the number of times you eat and all the places it occurs and you can understand the constant contribution of these spaces to halitosis.

Remember why teeth have food traps? I said that one of the causes is fillings or crowns that do not fit properly. If you have any areas of "open contacts", where food gets trapped, bring them to the attention of your dentist. If it is due to fillings or crowns not being tight enough, thus causing food to get trapped, it needs correction. Contacts between the teeth should be tight enough to "pop" when regular floss is pulled between the teeth. If you have food traps, to eliminate halitosis, bleeding, and gum disease, ***open contacts must be eliminated.***

Food traps also occur in the front or back of the teeth even when the contacts, which reside in the upper third of the teeth, are tight. This is because of *improper contours* of the teeth as they contact the adjacent teeth, such as a rotated tooth, an ill-fitting crown, or in gum disease. These too cause inflammation not to mention the fermentation of the food and resulting odors.

PROFESSIONAL TREATMENT

The basis of our professional treatment at the National Breath Center starts with the correct diagnosis. What I will share with you here are the diagnostic and treatment protocols we follow in our office. Please remember that actual treatment varies depending on the severity of the problem along with the other causative factors listed earlier.

THE DIAGNOSIS

Before we can make a diagnosis, we must establish a baseline from which all future data will be compared. This must occur before a person's first visit. If everyone follows the same protocol before their first appointment, we can then create comparisons on every diagnostic test to know how any single person varies from the baseline. This has been developed over 22 years with thousands of patients and allows me to make an accurate diagnosis by distinguishing tongue coatings, odors, and the results of other tests we use to determine if bad breath exists and how extensive it is.

To begin with, we ask each person to follow the Halitosis Pre-Appointment Protocol below. **The purpose of this Protocol is to eliminate any outside influences on mouth odor and allow the current odor to come through for an accurate diagnosis.**

HALITOSIS PRE-APPOINTMENT PROTOCOL

3 Days Before Examination:

Eliminate all spicy and odorous foods.
Stop any form of tongue hygiene.

2 Days Before Examination:

Stop the use of any mouthwash.

1 Day Before Examination:

Stop all oral hygiene. This includes tooth brushing, flossing, and mouthwash.

Day of Examination (if appointment is in AM):

Do not eat any food

DO NOT PERFORM ANY ORAL HYGIENE

Water is allowed. Please drink it only. Do not swish or rinse your mouth with it.

Day of Examination (if appointment is in PM):

Breakfast is allowed. Avoid spicy and odorous foods. DO NOT USE SALT.

DO NOT PERFORM ANY ORAL HYGIENE

Water is allowed. Please drink it only. Do not swish or rinse your mouth with it.

Bring a list of medications that you currently take to the office.

Do not use cologne, after shave, scented deodorants, or lotions the day of your appointment.

I understand that these instructions may create a hardship for some. However, to find the cause of your bad breath, we must create a baseline reading that tells us the degree of the problem.

If you are taking antibiotics, we will not be able to get accurate readings. You must wait three weeks after the end of the antibiotics to be evaluated.

INITIAL VISIT

When I see someone for the first time, I begin with a conversation about their problem. While it takes anywhere from 10-30 minutes, it is important for both of us to get a sense of what the problem is, what it means to the person, and what his or her past experiences have been. I simply begin by asking "How can I help you?" After their initial response, I go into a series of more specific questions to gather more information and delve into other important areas. Having done this for 22+ years, I know which road to take when people answer in different ways.

The following is a *partial list* of questions I ask my halitosis patients. Some are very simple, yet every answer gives me more information and ideas of how I can help. For example, "Do you do anything to treat your problem?"Their answer tells me about their oral hygiene care, what products someone is using, frequencies, times of hygiene, and effectiveness. For instance, if a response is "I floss my teeth," I am led to ask how frequently; how long does it take; do you ever smell the floss; have you ever seen blood on the floss; and other questions related to bad breath. This may sound like an exhaustive process, but to achieve a TOTAL CURE, I must know as much about what is being done as how severe the problem is. This is what allows me to design a Personal Professional Protocol for each patient.

HALITOSIS INITIAL INTERVIEW

Here are some of the questions I ask at the initial visit as I get to know the patient and their problem as best as can be known.

How do you know you that *YOU* have a problem with bad breath?

When did it start?

Do you also have a bad taste in your mouth?

Is the bad taste associated with the bad breath?

Is it worse at any time of the day?

Does anything make it better or make it worse?

What do you think is the cause of your problem?

Do you do anything to treat this problem?

Does your mouth often feel dry?

Do you have a history of sinus problems?

Respiratory problems?

Do you have a history of gastrointestinal problems?

Are you currently taking any medications?

Do you have any side-effects?

What is your typical diet like? (Colas, sweets, snacks?)

Does your food have an uncharacteristic taste?

Do you smoke? How frequently?

Are you a mouth breather?

Do you snore? Do you have sleep apnea?

Have you ever had a gum exam?

The questions above are general questions. I make them specific depending on the answers. One example that comes up frequently is about the relationship of bad breath and bad taste. A number of people assume that they have bad breath because they have a bad taste in their mouth (the most common tastes that I hear are "metallic" and "sour" tastes). This tells me that the person is actually tasting their own tongue biofilm.

COMPREHENSIVE ORAL EXAMINATION FOR HALITOSIS

The examination I perform would best be titled the **Comprehensive Examination for Halitosis + The Comprehensive Dental Examination.** Why? This is the only way I can know all the factors that are contributing to an individual's bad breath. For instance, x-rays tell us if there are ill-fitting fillings or crowns, food traps, root decay, decay between the teeth, abscessed teeth, bone loss, and other conditions that contribute to bad breath. A tooth examination can reveal decay, food traps, and ill-fitting dental work that contributes to bad breath as well as other information that may affect overall oral health. Of course, a gum examination tells if there are bleeding areas and any level of gum disease, should it exist. While I routinely do this as part of a comprehensive dental exam, it is also necessary as part of a halitosis examination. The goal is to be thorough in the diagnosis so personalized treatment can create a TOTAL CURE.

Let me tell you of a recent example. Upon examining a patient with halitosis, I noticed large open spaces between the teeth. Since he had not done any oral hygiene for 24 hours, I was also able to see the worst food traps and the areas of bacterial accumulation around the teeth. I also noted extreme wear on his teeth, even his front teeth, and many areas of abfraction (gum recession with bone loss and root exposure but no inflammation).

This indicated that he had a serious bite problem. The large spaces and food traps were not due to gum disease (inflammation) but the trauma of teeth hitting in the wrong places for a long time. This is why we do a thorough examination at the first visit.

I gauge the severity of halitosis using *four techniques*. Each gives me specific information about the problem and helps me form a personalized treatment plan. In addition, some of the procedures I use can also be used by each person to gauge their progress and monitor their mouth during and after treatment is complete. First, I take a Halimeter reading, which is the only method most dentists use. The Halimeter is a scientific instrument that measures the levels of VSCs in the breath. The reading is compared to a scale that I developed in 1995 and has been borne out by research. Then, I do the organoleptic test, a certified way of measuring bad breath and popular in scientific communities. Referred to as the "smell test," I ask the person to gently breathe on me as I put my nose close to their mouth. I ask them to repeat it with my nose about 6 inches away. Third, I wipe the back of their tongue 2-3 times with white, sterile gauze to see the color of the tongue coating underneath the top layers and rate its smell; the more discolored and the thicker the coating, the worse the problem. I photograph that gauze for our records and for later comparison during treatment. I also ask the person to tell me the color they see on the gauze and to smell the gauze themselves. I ask for their description, offer mine, and record the data. These four tests are necessary if one is to get the correct diagnosis.

As important as the Halimeter is for an objective number, it only measures hydrogen sulfide, and, using a

complex algorithm, extrapolates the other VSCs resulting in
a peak reading of Volatile Sulfur Compounds.

*However, if you refer to the chart I provided earlier, you
can see that there are other serious odor-causing compounds
that are not sulfur based, and thus not picked up by the
Halimeter.*

***Even though VSCs are the primary odor causing
compounds for about 80-90% of the people with bad breath,
the other people suffering from bad breath have more of a mix.
Combined with the characteristics of a biofilm, these people
have an odor that, while offensive, can best be discovered using
the other 3 tests we use at the National Breath Center.***

TREATMENT

After our initial examination of about 1½ hours is
complete, I then talk with each sufferer about a personalized
treatment program. It is important that they understand the
causes of their problem, how they can be cured, and how they
can regain control.

Remember The Big 4? Because of the primary need of
people coming for halitosis elimination, I divide treatment into
two phases.

Phase 1 is the immediate cure of the odor but not all
factors. That involves removal of the tongue biofilm and
treatment of the gums for bleeding and gum disease, and treating
suspected inadequate saliva flow. The number of visits varies
depending on the severity of the odor, the thickness of the

biofilm, the tenaciousness of the biofilm, and the gum component of treatment.

Of course, during the progression to the TOTAL CURE, I monitor each person for any changes and repeat all the diagnostic tests periodically to gauge progress. In addition, I keep photographic records of the tongue and the gauze as treatment progresses.

Phase 2 of the TOTAL CURE involves correction of dental problems that can contribute to bad breath such as places where food gets trapped.

The TOTAL CURE is straightforward: *no discernible bad breath* **using the 4 tests we use at the initial examination to diagnose halitosis.** The treatment is so effective that, if people do their part (home care and bad breath protocol) we have 100% cures rate.

In my office, if we have not achieved that goal, we add extra treatment at no charge until we are successful.

BENEFITS OF THE TOTAL CURE:
- ➤ NO DISCERNABLE BAD BREATH
- ➤ ELIMINATION OF TONGUE BIOFILM
- ➤ GUM DISEASE CURED OR CONTROLLED
- ➤ SCIENTIFIC MONITORING
- ➤ MODIFICATION OF TREATMENT BASED ON ONGOING RESULTS
- ➤ PERSONAL PROGRAM FOR HOME CARE
- ➤ A FRESH START

DURING & AFTER TREATMENT

My goal in the halitosis TOTAL CURE is *to eliminate the causes and odors of halitosis and make each person as self-sufficient as possible*. The techniques we use are **painless**. The TOTAL CURE does not rely on products to succeed. And, to maintain the cure we teach each patient *a personally modified Maintenance Protocol for their circumstances and their needs – to prevent the problem from returning*.

Once Phase 1 and Phase 2 are completed, what follows will maintain that cure.

TOTAL CURE: MAINTENANCE & PREVENTION

Here are the tools I recommend to my patients for ongoing maintenance and to keep bad breath from returning.

SUPREME BREATH™ Tru-ACTIVE ClO2 mouthrinse and toothpaste

Sonicare Flex Care Platinum toothbrush

Hydro Floss™ magnetic irrigator

Dry mouth patch (OraMoist Patch or Xylimelts): Xylitol gums or lozenges

Oral Probiotics with S. Salivarius K-12 and S.Salivarius M18

Gauze

Floss

Manual Brush (for travel)

Dentek Floss Pik, or other such device if needed for spaces between the teeth

Sinus Irrigator: Neti Pot or other device

The instruments, mouthrinse and toothpaste, and the techniques described later are all ones I use at the National Breath Center and have been using for years. While I am always open to new tools and techniques, I recommend these because they are all part of our TOTAL CURE program.

THE ULTIMATE ODOR & BACTERIA KILLER: *SUPREME BREATH™ Tru-ACTIVE CHLORINE DIOXIDE (ClO2)**

*There has been an important misconception regarding ACTIVE chlorine dioxide and "stabilized" chlorine dioxide, one that is not divulged on the advertiser's websites. While there are many brands that claim to contain ClO2, ones that call themselves "stabilized" ClO2 such as Therabreath, Oxyfresh, and Closys II, have virtually **NO** chlorine dioxide in them. **ACTIVE ClO2** is the only biocompatible chlorine dioxide compound that causes no injury to oral tissues while providing the most powerful level of bacterial kill and odor elimination.*

*For the record, "stabilized" ClO2 **is NOT chlorine dioxide at all and has no chlorine dioxide in it**.* Here's why. While the ***starting*** ingredient in both "stabilized" ClO2 and ACTIVE chlorine dioxide is chlorite, the chemical process for making "stabilized" ClO2 adds one or more salts and hydrogen peroxide to the chlorite *which only stabilizes the chlorite.* In essence, "stabilized" chlorine dioxide is stabilized *chlorite.* **This process does not create ACTIVE ClO2**. To do this, the chlorite must be ACTIVATED.

SUPREME BREATH™ Tru-ACTIVE ClO2 products are worlds apart from such products misnamed "stabilized" ClO2. To make Tru-ACTIVE ClO2, a mild acid is mixed with chlorite that slowly releases the ACTIVE chlorine dioxide gas, which is immediately *captured in a liquid or gel like the carbonation in soda,* In this case, it is captured in the mouthwash and toothpaste. Tru-ACTIVE ClO2 releases chlorine dioxide at a physiologic pH, close to the pH of saliva, and optimized for use in the oral cavity. To do this, Tru-ACTIVE ClO2 is provided in two separate containers to be *mixed on demand*. This is the characteristic that makes Tru-ACTIVE ClO2 so powerful.

How does SUPREME BREATH™ Tru-ACTIVE ClO2 work? When mixed, oxygen is released in a **VERY ACTIVE** state - it attaches itself to the VSCs and other odor-causing molecules, and changes their chemical composition immediately, thus eliminating the odor. Its extraordinary bacteria kill rate occurs because it breaks the bacterial cell wall of the bacteria that are the cause of mouth odor and gum disease. Since human cells do not have cell walls like bacteria, human tissue is not affected so *it is non-toxic and the bacteria cannot build up any resistance to Tru-ACTIVE ClO2.*

And, ***here's the most incredible property of SUPREME BREATH™ Tru-ACTIVE ClO2****: <u>**you can regulate its strength to suit your specific needs by changing the time before use.**</u> You can control the strength of your mouthwash, and, for the protocols mentioned later, such as the gauze protocol, irrigation,*

A different ACTIVE ClO2 product (ProFresh™) is fixed at one concentration and cannot be used at other concentrations needed for different applications. It also lasts a limited amount of time, tastes like bleach, and does not allow you to vary its strength. For example, using Tru-ACTIVE ClO2 allows you to create **full strength activity** in the water irrigator to kill the bacteria and odors under the gums by mixing 20ml of each solution (8 teaspoons) into the reservoir of water. Its dilution strength is the most powerful there is. ProFresh users must use about 8 ounces, ½ a bottle, to create the same concentration. So for those of you who have gum disease, the most effective means to irrigate under the gums is the Hydro Floss instrument and you need much less Supreme Breath Mouthrinse to accomplish the task.

*Another top advantage is that the solution **destroys anaerobic bacteria - the ones that cause gum disease,** and is a mainstay in our office for gum disease patients. Over the years, I have seen that Tru-ACTIVE ClO2 surpasses Peridex, the most commonly recommended and used rinse for gum disease by periodontists.*

SUPREME BREATH™ Tru-ACTIVE ClO2*

- *Instantly eliminates bad breath*
- *NOT a cover-up*
- *Oxidizes VSCs to neutralize odor*
- *100% bacterial kill rate in 30 seconds*
- *Kills bacteria that cause halitosis*
- *Kills bacteria and maintains healthy gums*
- *Loosens biofilm (coating) on tongue and teeth*
- *Helps protect enamel*
- *Non-toxic*
- *Tastes great*
- *Does not stain the teeth*
- *Research tested*

How do you know if your product is **ACTIVE** or "stabilized"? **ACTIVE ClO2 *must be mixed*** from two solutions to create the bacterial killing properties and odor killing effects. ***It cannot reside in one bottle*** like so-called "stabilized" ClO2. And, with Tru-ACTIVE ClO2 mixed on demand, each separate part has a long shelf life.

One word about advertising. The products mentioned above, Therabreath, Oxyfresh, Closys II, and ProFresh, all advertise that they have a **CURE**. However, ***because they must be used every day or many times a day, they are not a cure.*** Remember the definition of a cure?

A CURE should eliminate the problem itself, all related causes, and provide the means to keep halitosis from coming back.

From testing and experience, I believe **SUPREME BREATH™ Tru-ACTIVE Chlorine Dioxide (ClO2)** is the best ACTIVE Chlorine Dioxide product on the market. I personally use it, give it to my patients as part of the TOTAL CURE, and recommend it for maintenance, the Beating Bad Breath Protocol©, prevention of halitosis, and as the best mouthwash available. I also use it to keep gum problems in check and to help prevent the tongue biofilm from forming again in people who have experienced the CURE. It is the *True Bacteria and Odor Killer*.

THE BEST TOOTHBRUSH

The one toothbrush that I have used exclusively for almost two decades has a higher degree of success than anything else I have tried.

The Sonicare Flexcare Platinum toothbrush is a toothbrush that vibrates, thus allowing the brush to remove more biofilm - plaque and bacteria. When placed near a 45-degree angle to the tooth and gum line, using short rather than scrubbing movements, it easily covers a far greater surface area that any other brush. I personally use this and have been recommending it since my first book in 1995. The reason I prefer the Sonicare is that with minimum effort, it will cover the maximum surface areas of your teeth and gums. The reason I prefer this version is because it has a "gentle" setting. This setting does not create sensitive teeth but has the right amount of speed and sonic action to do a great job at cleaning the teeth and gums.

One more important point about the Sonicare. It has a timer that vibrates every 30 seconds, making it ideal to spend that amount of time on each quarter of the mouth. And after 2 minutes of brushing, it automatically turns itself off.

THE BEST ORAL IRRIGATOR

I believe that the number one irrigator for oral health is the **HydroFloss™**. Why do I believe it to be the best irrigator? Because its magnetic technology alters the molecules and helps removes more debris from teeth surfaces.

The HydroFloss is the best delivery system to get Tru-ACTIVE ClO2 under the gums to kill the bacteria, eliminate the compounds that cause gum disease, and help eliminate the bleeding, thus leading to less gum disease and less odor. I personally use the HydroFloss and recommend it in the office. I use a setting of 3-4. That is all that is needed.

However, it is important to remember that any biofilm, like that attached to the teeth, its roots, and under the gums, can only be removed by mechanical means. So, to make this instrument effective, it is important to first, dislodge the biofilm with floss, and then kill the bacteria and odors around the teeth with the HydroFloss and the Tru-Active ClO2.

DRY MOUTH PRODUCTS

As my studies with patients continued, I realized that to create the TOTAL CURE, there had to be a missing ingredient. That problem is a dry mouth.

Most people don't even know they have this problem and certainly do not reveal it during my extensive interview. So I began to simply observe the people over a one year period that had what I believed to be a less than adequate saliva flow to wash away the continuously accumulating debris. I was not looking to diagnose a medical condition. I was looking for people that had less saliva than my regular dental patients. What I discovered was a far greater number than I anticipated.

So as not to disturb any medication they were taking, I used OTC products to try to stimulate saliva flow. One I recommend is **OraMoist Dry Mouth Patches**. Not only does it work at night when saliva naturally stops and we need it more than ever, it does not interfere with the day-time protocol. Other recommendations I make for those with less than adequate saliva are **Xylitol** brand products (gums and lozenges) and sipping out of a cup during the day. If you cannot find the Xylitol brand be sure that what you purchase has no artificial ingredients. Another alternative would be **Xylimelt** wafers, however, they are cumbersome to use at night, but can be used to supplement the patch during the day.

ORAL PROBIOTICS

As research has progressed, one track that has proved useful is that of helping add more strains of "good" bacteria to crowd out the "bad" bacteria. Currently, products are being marketed that contain the two most important strains of bacteria – *S. Salivarius K12* and *S. Salivarius M18*.

These probiotics only work on the top layers of the biofilm and not the middle or lower layers where most of the odor comes from so they have limited efficacy. However, if the biofilm has been professionally eliminated, they are a useful product for keeping the biofilm from re-forming.

At the National Breath Center we have tested many brands and currently use a product made by hyperbiotics (company name) called Pro-Dental. This product has the most live bacteria available making it the most effective. It is recommended for all patients once treatment is complete.

FLOSS

Flossing is by far the best technique that removes the biofilm – bacteria, bacterial food, dead cells, and debris - from between the teeth. If you remember from earlier, a **biofilm** must be removed by mechanical action. *The biofilm must be mechanically detached so the right products can neutralize them.*

I personally use **Deep Clean Ultra Floss®** by Oral B. It has a section of yarn-like material in the center, thus giving it a much greater surface area to remove the bacteria.

For hard-to-get to areas, I recommend the **Dentek Floss Pik®** or a similar brand. These are particularly useful for limited dexterity, places you cannot reach, and for those with arthritis. Shaped like a hoe, the front part that is bent down has a piece of floss attached. It allows a person to maneuver the pik with one hand instead of two, making it easy to use. By the way, another good thing about the floss pik and similar products is that they are easy to hide in any pocket or purse and can be used after a meal or anytime. I also have patients use the **GUM Soft-Picks®** for spaces between the teeth. Other brands exist, and you may find one more to your liking.

Here are the principles of flossing: (a) use what works to really clean out the biofilm between the teeth; (b) use the correct flossing technique; and (c) spend the time to floss thoroughly between and behind the teeth.

GAUZE

Personal cleaning of the tongue with a long-standing biofilm coating is an impossible task, as the coatings are too deep and too thick. With the TOTAL CURE, everyone has a clean tongue so patients only need maintenance. It is partly done with gauze and SUPREME BREATH™ Tru-ACTIVE ClO2.

Until now, tongue scrapers have been recommended as the treatment of choice. However, tongue scrapers are only able to remove yesterday's layer. People with chronic bad breath need much more removed. Remember – biofilms can only be removed by mechanical means. That is why those 99.7% cures, the magic secrets, and most products on the internet are false claims. Some of the people I see have even injured their tongues while using a tongue scraper.

Gauze is the best tongue cleaner that allows you to scrub the tongue, especially when the correct mouthwash is added for deeper penetration to lower coatings, instead of only the top layers, as tongue scrapers do. It is the only mechanical action that allows you to eliminate deeper than the last layer that formed. And it is the best tongue cleaning agent that I ever found. Gauze and Tru-ACTIVE ClO2 are a cornerstone of our Maintenance Program and the Beating Bad Breath Protocol.

SINUS IRRIGATOR AND MORNING BREATH

If you're like me, I wake up with morning breath and can taste it from the back of my throat. This is one indication of my allergies and dry mouth. Allergies produce the phlegm, and a dry mouth at night complicates it.

Many years ago, I began using a **Neti Pot** sold at many pharmacies, health food stores, and on the internet. I use it before I go to sleep and when I wake in the morning. Now the effects of those issues on my breath are no longer noticeable. The Neti Pot flushes away bacteria and prevents mucous from forming in my throat and on the lingual tonsils. Now I can be assured that there will be no sinus odor the entire day.

PERSONALIZED CARE

If experience has taught me anything, it is that each sufferer of bad breath is different. While each may have The Big 4 components of halitosis, even all 6 factors, not only is the severity of each different, causing a variation of the protocol, but the people and their circumstances are different.

Just imagine the differences between an office worker who fears getting close to co-workers or sitting next to people in meetings; being afraid of getting a promotion or even keeping his or her job; or a salesperson whose breath makes it a necessity to stand back from people lest they get offended and lose the sale; or a bride-to-be whose wedding is about to be called off. All not only have a different set of circumstances, emotions, and fears, they all react differently to their circumstances and their cure. In our office we make it a point to treat each person individually, with respect, empathy, and superior technical skills.

At the National Breath Center, our goals are not simply to eliminate bad breath, but to help eliminate anxiety, help people know that their problem is solved, and increase their confidence, and to give people the techniques to keep it from coming back.

THERE IS A CURE FOR HALITOSIS!!

THE MAINTENANCE PROGRAM

Anyone who has had the TOTAL CURE should refer to their Personal Maintenance Protocol document your doctor will have already completed for your personal care.

In addition, **the maintenance protocol is the BEST TREATMENT you can use for excellent oral health and to PREVENT BAD BREATH.**

For those who have experienced the CURE, since you are starting with a non-coated tongue, gum disease cured or in control, spaces closed, and food traps eliminated, here are the general guidelines to maintain the TOTAL CURE:

Upon awakening:
Remove dry mouth patch (if used)
Drink a full glass of cool water. Sip 6-8 glasses per day to wash away bacteria and to help create saliva.

After breakfast:
- Floss
- If allergies, sinus problems, post-nasal drip, or the accumulation of mucous or phlegm are a problem, use a NetiPot or other device per instructions
- Brush with **SUPREME BREATH™ Tru-ACTIVE ClO2 toothpaste** with the Sonicare for 2 minutes – 30 seconds on each quarter of your mouth
- Saturate **3 gauze** with Tru – ACTIVE ClO2 mouthrinse solution.

Because it is in two parts, place 4-5 squirts of each in a cup, enough to saturate the gauze with some extra for swishing, wait 30 seconds, then put the gauze in the mixture and move it around and between your fingers to properly mix it inside the cup for about 30 seconds. Squeeze out the gauze and keep the extra for swishing in a minute (see below); Wait another 1 minute to use. Just remember that the gauze should be thoroughly mixed and saturated but not dripping before use.

- Wipe your tongue, especially the back, in every direction for 10 seconds. Do this with the 6 sides of the 3 gauze, wiping the remainder of the top surface. Be aggressive. I have never had anyone hurt themselves using this technique. Do not be concerned if you gag. While unpleasant, even I gag when I use this technique
- With the excess form the cup, rinse and gargle 2 minutes *with the remainder of the solution*
- If recommended by your doctor fill the HydroFloss with a full reservoir of water; then mix 20ml of each solution of Tru-ACTIVE Cl02 in a cup and wait 10 minutes after mixing before placing in the irrigator (this creates the optimal strength even when diluted by the water); Irrigate your whole mouth around the teeth and gums;
- Apply Dry Mouth Patch if indicated by your doctor

Before bed: Repeat full regimen above as after breakfast.
Apply dry mouth patch for nighttime use.

During the day: Vary treatment depending on your needs as described below. At the very least, do the gauze wipes after lunch and rinse if possible.

- Over the years, I have found that the *BEST technique to remove mouth odor during the day and to keep the tongue coating from building up,* is to first, use gauze saturated with SUPREME BREATH™ Tru-ACTIVE ClO2 from the portable **CONFIDENCE PUMP BOTTLE** and second, rinse and gargle with Tru-ACTIVE ClO2 mouthwash. You can carry the bottle with you
- Because the Confidence Pump bottle sprays out both solutions separately, simply spray enough solution to saturate 3 gauze and move the gauze between the fingers for 30 seconds before using. Wait 1-2 minutes. Then aggressively scrub your tongue multiple times, using both sides of the gauze. For maximum results repeat with different gauze. Remember that scrubbing action removes more of the tongue biofilm and once CURED, you will be preventing the biofilm (coating) from coming back.
- Use Pro-Dental probiotics to maintain the level of "good bacteria" helping keep the biofilm layer from re-forming

In addition, if you want extra protection, instead of mixing the Supreme Breath solution in a separate container, you can easily spray the Confidence Pump bottle 4-8 times in your mouth and swish it everywhere for 2 minutes (the number of sprays should be enough to amply swish and gargle with it).The swishing mixes the two solutions and creates the right concentration for a touchup.

These two techniques in combination have become the primary ones I recommend to people for daytime use in the Maintenance Program. Here is why: You eliminate more tongue coating, you use less product, it is easy to carry, do quickly, and dispose of. It is the best way to kill bacteria and remove the odor causing molecules.

REMEMBER: THE PURPOSE OF THE GAUZE TECHNIQUE IS TO KEEP BIOFILM FROM FORMING AT THE LOWER DEPTHS OF THE TONGUE AFTER MEALS AND/OR DURING THE DAY

If you have a **dry mouth**, or a mouth without adequate saliva, use the products mentioned above to help hydrate your mouth. If you have **sinus issues or allergies**, gargle with the mouthrinse in addition to swishing with it.

If you have these conditions, I would also recommend use of a saline solution nasal spray. Two I particularly like are the Ocean brand and Nutri-Biotic Nasal Spray Plus. Ocean is a saline solution that simulates the flushing of the nasal passages. To do that during the day, I spray enough up one nostril so that it acts as a NetiPot but with less liquid. The Nutri-Biotic product, however, adds an extra antiseptic ingredient to be even more effective if you use it simply for a nasal spray. I do not use it for a nasal flush. You will not find me without one or the other during allergy season.

If you have **food traps**, find a product like the Dentek Floss Pick or some similar flossing device that you can carry in a purse or pocket to remove the food easily and quickly. And see your dentist to correct these food traps and open spaces. These spaces can cause gum disease or make it worse and create the food traps where bacteria go wild. If your dentist tells you not to worry about the food traps, find another dentist.

At the National Breath Center, we routinely close the spaces with fillings that are broader and tighter to the next tooth.

No matter which techniques you use, **SUPREME BREATH™ Tru -ACTIVE ClO2** will kill the halitosis bacteria and eliminate their odor-causing molecules.

PART VII

PERSONAL TREATMENT

WHAT YOU CAN DO

The correct professional protocol is the cure for bad breath. It is the only way to eliminate all the biofilms existing on the tongue and around the teeth that cause halitosis and give someone a fresh start.

However, for those who cannot find a dentist certified in halitosis elimination or cannot afford to, the **Beating Bad Breath Protocol**© is a proven technique to kill bacteria and neutralize odors. Even though many companies advertise a 12-hour cure, 99.9% results, or some other promise in a bottle, these are all advertising gimmicks. The longevity of the effectiveness of any product depends on the size and thickness of the tongue biofilm (coating), your tongue anatomy, the activity of the bacteria inside the coating, the food you eat, how fast you re-accumulate the biofilm, whether you have gum disease and how serious, and the amount and longevity of fermenting food in the food traps. It also depends on whether your products are ACTIVE or stabilized chlorine dioxide.

The purpose of the **Beating Bad Breath Protocol** is to CONFIDENTLY put **YOU** back in control of your problem and to eliminate the anxiety of being around others. While this is not a cure, it is the best, tested alternative.

While the products here are the same as the Maintenance Protocol, don't forget to read Part VI: THE PROFESSIONAL APPROACH: THE TOTAL CURE. That chapter covers in detail the tools to use and how to use them.

Halitosis has been different in every one of the over 7,000 people I have seen. Just as their stories differ, the quantity, the quality, the ease of removal, and the psycho-social effects similarly vary. Thus, as much as I'd like there to be, experience has taught me there is no "one size fits all" answer. *The protocols, suggestions, and insights I offer you are meant to tip the scale of bad breath to your control. In other words, you no longer need to be a victim of something you do not have control over. So it is essential that each person using the information in this book try it and modify it according to their results. It takes practice and observation on your part. But, if you do accept the responsibility for your own care, I believe you will find the way that works the best for you*. Here are the tools you will need to be successful.

BEATING BAD BREATH PROTOCOL TOOLS

SUPREME BREATH™ Tru-ACTIVE ClO2 mouthrinse and toothpaste

SUPREME BREATH™ Tru-ACTIVE ClO2 Confidence Pump Bottle

Sonicare™ Flex Care Toothbrush

HydroFloss™ irrigator

Probiotics with S. Salivarius K12 and S. Salivarius M18

Dry mouth patch (**OraMoist Patch**), Xylitol products, Xylimelts

Gauze 2" x 2"

Floss

Manual Brush (for travel or work)

Floss Pik or other tools if needed for spaces between the teeth

Sinus Irrigator: NetiPot

INTRODUCTION TO THE
BEATING BAD BREATH PROTOCOL©

The Beating Bad Breath Protocol is presented with the understanding that the people that use this still have a tongue biofilm (coating) and may have different levels of gum disease. **This protocol is not a cure but a way to gain control of halitosis so you can feel confident again.** Again, gum disease is a serious condition and I strongly recommend that you see a dentist for proper diagnosis and gum treatment if needed.

In addition to the protocol, **I must strongly recommend that you eliminate the foods listed earlier and stop smoking**. Even coffee and tea can cause thicker coatings and odors, and need to be removed before you can actually begin to remove the long-term coatings. Every one of those foods fortifies the bacteria or thickens the biofilm on the tongue increasing the coating and making it impossible for you to get control of your problem.

Here's how to make the **Beating Bad Breath Protocol** work for you.

To begin, you need to establish a baseline as I do in my office, so that you can compare future results.

Before you start, find someone who cares enough about you to be your guide. Friend, relative, child, spouse—it does not matter. (Spouses may not be the best guides as they do not want to hurt your feelings. In addition, they would be the one person who has adapted the most to our problem.) Ask them if they will help you through a difficult time as you work to get your bad breath under control. Find a notebook to record your results and then start with the following steps.

Before you use any of the products or tools and before you use any oral hygiene techniques, 3 hours after you awake, without having breakfast and before any oral hygiene practices, ask your guide to lean in close and gently breathe on them. Ask them to rate your breath on a scale from 1-10, 10 being the worst odor they have smelled. Record it in a notebook, *but do not get discouraged.* We are looking for a baseline that is a starting point **only**, not a judgment about you. During my halitosis examination, I ask patients to do the same even though I also smell their breath (organoleptic reading).

Second, after they have smelled your breath, take a 2" x 2" gauze and aggressively wipe your tongue as far back as you can reach, 3-4 times. If your mouth is appreciably dry, take a sip of water first. Describe the color in your notebook. Then ask them to describe the color and make the notes in your notebook. *It is important that you do these first and do not discuss them with your guide so they are not influenced by your own perceptions.*

One minute after you take the gauze out, smell the coating. While I commonly use the terms "sour," "pungent," and "strong" I urge you to use a scale of 1-10 with 10 being the worst odor you have ever smelled. Then ask your guide to describe the odor. Write their description in your notebook. Be aware that not everyone can smell their own gauze. It is one more manifestation of adaption, that sensory phenomenon mentioned earlier.

As your treatment progresses, repeat this testing once per week. After a few weeks, you will be using the protocol regularly, so be sure to test 3-4 hours after your last use for an accurate reading. You are looking for improvement. Do they notice a difference? Do you?

It may be some time before the gauze will change color or odor as you will still have a majority of the original coating. What you need is perseverance. As time goes on you will see a change in the gauze tests. Your goal is to create that change over time.

At first, *the primary test to use as you treat yourself is the smell test. That is what your guide will notice getting better.* **And this is where your guide must be honest with you.**

Note: What we are looking for is not a cure, but a treatment that works. That is why you will need to modify your protocol to get it to work for you. You can increase treatment with the gauze and/or rinse; you can eliminate food from between the teeth before it begins to ferment - before odor is created; you can brush during the day; and you can modify daytime treatment as needed. **SUPREME BREATH™ Tru-ACTIVE ClO2** is non-toxic and neither you nor the bacteria can build up any immunity to it. ***My goal for you is to use this Protocol so thoroughly that you will need the least amount of touchup during the day.***

Without professional gas monitors we cannot get objective numbers. But your friends and family do not care about numbers. They care about your well-being. So, using your Guide, test after you have given any change you make a chance to work for *at least one week* to determine if it has changed your breath. DO NOT change what you do every few days. Have patience.

One more note. Here's how to know if you have less than adequate saliva. Three to four hours after you eat, take a finger and place it under your tongue. Is it extremely wet? Partly wet? Dry? The dryer your finger is, the dryer your mouth is. Run this test to determine if you need to add a saliva enhancer to your own protocol. This may be one of the most important steps you take. And if you are just not sure, then try the saliva enhancing products anyway.

USING THE BEATING BAD BREATH TREATMENT PROTOCOL

The goal of The Beating Bad Breath Protocol is to put *you* in control of your breath problem, no longer a victim to it, and to increase your confidence that you will be confident in social situations without the cover-up odors that scream, "I have bad breath". With the right techniques and your own monitoring as above, you can regain the confidence you have lost.

The Beating Bad Breath Treatment Protocol© with SUPREME BREATH™ Tru-ACTIVE ClO2 is NOT a cover-up. Why? Because you are killing the bacteria, destroying the odor, helping gingivitis and gum disease, and even removing some of the tongue coating. For some people the morning protocol lasts until bedtime with assistance from the saliva enhancers during the day and night. For others, they will need patience to discover the best regimen for them using some of the modifications noted here. DO NOT GIVE UP! I have never found a person who did not find the right way for them.

Beating Bad Breath Protocol©

Upon awakening: Remove dry mouth patch (if dry mouth)
Drink a full glass of cool water. Drink 6-8 glasses per day to wash away bacteria and increase saliva or sip the water continuously

After breakfast:

- Floss
- If allergies, sinus problems, post-nasal drip, or the accumulation of mucous or phlegm are a problem, use a NetiPot
- Brush with **SUPREME BREATH™ Tru-ACTIVE ClO2** toothpaste with the Sonicare for 2 minutes
- Saturate 3 gauze with Tru – ACTIVE ClO2 mouthrinse solution.
    > Because it is in two parts, place 5 squirts of each in a cup, enough to saturate the gauze; wait 30 seconds, then put the gauze in the mixture and move it around and between your fingers to properly mix it inside the cup for about 30 seconds. Wait another 1 minute to use. (if this is too strong, you can wait a shorter time interval; Squeeze the excess liquid out of the gauze.
- Wipe your tongue, especially the back, in every direction for 10 seconds. Repeat with each side of the 3 gauze also wiping the remainder of the

top surface. Be aggressive. I have never had anyone hurt themselves using this technique

- Fill the HydroFloss with a full reservoir of water; then mix 20ml of each solution of Tru-ACTIVE Cl02 in a cup and wait 10 minutes after mixing before placing in the irrigator; irrigate your whole mouth around the teeth and gums. This creates the optimal strength even when diluted by the water
- Rinse and gargle 2 minutes with the remaining Tru-ACTIVE ClO2 mouthwash in the gauze cup
- Use saliva enhancing products

Mid-Morning & Mid-Afternoon: Vary treatment depending on your needs. *Do all or at least the first two together.* These directions assume that you are using the Confidence Pump bottle. The CONFIDENCE PUMP bottle is a unique spray bottle that is easily carried in a pocket or purse and dispenses both solutions of ClO2 at the same time to create Tru-ACTIVE ClO2. It can be used to saturate the gauze and as a mouthrinse.

- Saturate 3 gauze by squirting enough solution into the gauze; move the wet gauze between your fingers for 1 minute to mix the two solutions;
- Scrub your tongue all over using both sides of each gauze (6 sides)
- Use the **CONFIDENCE PUMP BOTTLE** with SUPREME BREATH Tru – ACTIVE ClO2 mouthrinse by squirting 4-8 squirts directly into your mouth; rinse and gargle with this mix for 2 minutes

- Follow instructions below for dry mouth, sinus problems or allergies, food traps and other problems
- Add Pro-Dental probiotics as needed

Because the Supreme Breath products are non-toxic, you cannot repeat these procedures too often. Just do what you need to regain your confidence. You have control of how often to use them and their concentration based on what works for you.

After Lunch:

- Floss; use other instruments for food traps
- Brush with manual brush you carry with you using same technique as with Sonicare (2 minutes)

Do at least two of the techniques below

- Saturate 3 gauze and scrub your tongue all over with both sides of the 3 gauze (6 sides)
- Use CONFIDENCE PUMP BOTTLE with Tru-ACTIVE ClO2 mouthrinse (see above)
- Rinse and gargle 2 minutes with 4-8 squirts of Tru-ACTIVE ClO2 mouthwash from the Confidence Pump bottle
- Follow instructions below for dry mouth, sinus problems or allergies, food traps and other problems below

Before bed: Repeat full regimen above as after breakfast. Apply dry mouth patch for nighttime use if indicated. An alternative is to use Xylimelts between the cheeks and gum on both sides

Over the years, I have found that the *BEST techniques to remove mouth odor during the day* is to first, use gauze saturated with SUPREME BREATH™ Tru-ACTIVE ClO2 from the CONFIDENCE PUMP Bottle and second, rinse and gargle with Tru-ACTIVE ClO2 mouthwash.

Simply spray enough solution to saturate the gauze and move it between the fingers for 30 seconds before using. Wait 1-2 minutes. Then aggressively scrub your tongue multiple times, using both sides of the gauze. For maximum results, repeat 6 times with both sides of 3 gauze. You can use it as often as you like during the day and it can be done at your desk or most other places and the gauze easily discarded. Remember that the scrubbing action removes more of the tongue biofilm.

In addition, instead of mixing the solution in a separate container, you can easily use the Confidence Pump Bottle 4-8 sprays in your mouth and swish it everywhere for 2 minutes (the number of sprays should be enough to amply swish and gargle with it).The swishing mixes the two solutions and creates the right concentration for a touchup.

In combination, these two techniques are the primary ones I recommend to people for daytime use in the Maintenance Program and the Beating Bad Breath Protocol. Here is why: You eliminate more tongue coating, you use less product, and it is easy to hide, do quickly, and dispose of. It is the best way to kill bacteria and remove the odor causing molecules. For best results, use the two techniques together.

However, you may need more depending on your tongue coating and amount of gum problems. Here is a ***stronger*** *rinse technique, the* same one used in the morning and before bed:

place equal amounts of SUPREME BREATH Tru-ACTIVE ClO2, 5 squirts of each solution in a cup, swirl for about thirty seconds in the cup, and swish after 4-5 minutes. The longer you wait, the stronger it gets. *In general, the concentration will continue to rise for about 10 minutes and then decrease.*

Use the amount that works for you, remembering that you want to get it into every area in your mouth and gargle with it. Moreover, if you have any sinus problems, allergies, or mucous, this renews the bacteria-killing action and neutralization of the odor-causing volatile sulfur compounds in the throat.

If you have a **dry mouth**, a mouth without adequate saliva, apply another dry mouth patch after lunch or use the saliva enhancers during the day. If you have **sinus issues or allergies**, gargle with the mouthrinse in addition to swishing with it.

If you have any type of sinus issue, I would also recommend use of a saline solution nasal spray. Two I particularly like are the Ocean brand and Nutri-Biotic Nasal Spray Plus. Ocean is a saline solution that simulates the flushing of the nasal passages. To do that during the day, I spray enough up one nostril so that it acts as a NetiPot but with less liquid. The Nutri-Biotic product, however, adds an extra antiseptic ingredient to be even more effective if you use it simply for a nasal spray. I do not use it for a nasal flush. You will not find me without one or the other during allergy season.

If your allergies or sinus problems are particularly miserable, consider taking the NetiPot with you to the office. It is not the most attractive thing to carry but it gets the job done.

If you have **food traps**, find a product like the Dentek Floss Pick or some similar flossing device that you can put in a pocket to remove the food easily and quickly. And see your dentist to correct these food traps and open spaces. For gum disease alone, they are either making it worse, or starting it.

I know how difficult it is to follow a comprehensive regimen during the workday. However, the more you scrub your tongue, the more coating you remove. And, when you add the mouthrinse at the same time, you kill even more bacteria and odors. You cannot get immune to SUPREME BREATH™ Tru-ACTIVE ClO2 so use it as you wish.

WHAT YOU CAN EXPECT

It is perfectly understandable that during the first part of this program you will not feel confident that you are in control. When you begin, to keep your confidence high, feel free to use the rinse and the tongue gauze protocol as much as you feel necessary for any situations that previously caused you distress. When to use them is up to you. As you find that the Tru-ACTIVE CLO2 really works best and that you have the tools and techniques for an occasional touchup, you will need the daytime additions less and less.

No matter which techniques you use, **SUPREME BREATH™ Tru-ACTIVE ClO2** will protect you better than anything else on the market. If your problem is chronic, seemingly unsolvable, or if you want a start fresh, you will need professional care as discussed in the previous chapter.

HOW TO FIND A DENTIST
WHO KNOWS THE TOTAL CURE

At the time of this writing, there is no list of dentists certified in successful halitosis treatment and cure. One list, American Breath Specialists, lists all dentists no matter their treatment. As I mentioned earlier, most dentists have gone to selling products and call that a cure. This is the list I used to survey dentists, however, it is a good place to start to find a dentist who knows the cure.

As I researched this book, I called over 30 dental offices and breath clinics that advertised bad breath elimination as a service they provide, to see what type of treatment they provided. Here are the questions I asked. If you locate someone, I suggest that you ask these also:

Does your office treat bad breath?
How many people do you treat each year?
Can you tell me something about how it is done?
What methods does the doctor use to diagnose my problem?
Do I have any treatment from the doctor?
Can you tell me what the treatment is?
How long does it take?
Is there any follow up?

These questions should tell you much about how treatment is done in that office. When the nurse at one so-called "specialist's" office told me that I would not receive any direct treatment from the doctor, that I would leave with the products I needed, and that I probably would not need to return as I'd be cured by the next day, I knew that this doctor did not know how to cure halitosis and just sold products.

And, if you cannot find a dentist you may want to consider traveling to the National Breath Center outside Washington, DC. We see people from all over the country each week and go out of our way to accommodate their schedule. We also offer discounts to those who make the trip by airplane.

The Appendix

In updating the research for the first version of this book, I studied numerous research papers as listed below. Since the Total Cure is 100% effective, I searched for papers that mentioned our clinical treatment, however, I could not find any. Combined with the research I did by calling numerous dental offices who said they specialized in curing bad breath, I found that the National Breath Center is the only facility that totally removes the biofilm and guarantees the cure of bad breath.

Testimonials

I have included some testimonials here from actual patients we have treated in the recent past. They are all unsolicited and come from people whose lives were changed having the Total Cure.

Medications

The list of medications is long since there are so many that dry the mouth. It is important to note that if you are taking any medication that dries the mouth you need saliva enhancers to counteract the drying effects of these medications. This holds true even if your dry mouth is only occasional, perhaps for a few hours after you take the medication. Experiment with the suggestions mentioned previously and find the best products that work for you.

APPENDIX A
BIBLIOGRAPHY

References

Ademovski, S. E., Persson, G. R., Winkel, E., Tangerman, A., Lingstrom, P., & Renvert, S. (2012). The short-term treatment effects on the microbiota at the dorsum of the tongue in intra-oral halitosis patients-a randomized clinical trial. *Clinical Oral Investigation*.

Amano, A., Yoshida, Y., Oho, T., & Koga, T. (2002). Monitoring ammonia to assess halitosis1. *Oral Surgery, Oral Medicine, Oral Pathology, Oral Radiology & Endodontics, 94*(6), 692-696. doi: 10.1067/moe.2002.126911

Awano, S., Koshimune, S., Kurihara, E., Gohara, K., Sakai, A., Soh, I., ... Takehara, T. (2004). The assessment of methyl mercaptan, an important clinical marker for the diagnosis of oral malodor. *Journal of Dentistry, 32*(7), 555-559. doi: 10.1016/j.jdent.2004.06.001

Begum, M., & McKenna, P. J. (2011). Olfactory reference syndrome: A systematic review of the world literature. *Psychological Medicine, 41*(3), 453-461.

Berg, M., & Fosdick, L. (1946). Studies in periodontal disease: II. Putrefactive organisms in the mouth. *Journal of Dental Research, 25*, 73-81.

Berg, M., Burrill, D. Y., & Fosdick, L. S. (1946). Chemical studies in periodontal disease III: Putrefaction of salivary proteins. *Journal of Dental Research, 25*, 231-246.

Blankenhorn, M. A., & Richards, C. E. (1936). Garlic breath odor. *Journal of the American Medical Association, 107*(6), 409-410.

Borden, L. C., Chaves, E. S., Bowman, J. P., Fath, B. M., & Hollar, G. L. (2002). The effect of four mouthrinses on oral malodor. *Compendium of Continuing Education in Dentistry, 23*(6), 531-536, 538, 540.

Bornstein, M. M., Kislig, K., Hoti, B. B., Seemann, R., & Lussi, A. (2009). Prevalence of halitosis in the population of the city of Bern, Switzerland:. *European Journal of Oral Sciences, 117*(3), 261-267. doi: 10.1111/j.1600-0722.2009.00630.x

Bosch, M., Nart, J., Audivert, S., Bonachera, M. A., Alemany, A. S., Fuentes, M. C., & Cune, J. (2012). Isolation and characterization of probiotic strains for improving oral health. *Archive of Oral Biology, 57*(5), 539-549.

Bosy, A. (1997). Oral malodor: Philosophical and practical aspects. *Journal of the Canadian Dental Association, 63*(3), 105-106.

Bosy, A., Kulkarni, G. V., Rosenberg, M., & McCulloch, C. (1994). Relationship of oral malodor to periodontitis: Evidence of independence in discrete subpopulations. *Journal of Periodontology, 65*(1), 37-46. doi: 10.1902/jop.1994.65.1.37

Braun, R. E., & Cianco, S. G. (1992). Subgingival delivery by an oral irrigation device. *Journal of Periodontology, 63*, 469-472.

Brening, R. H., Sulser, G. F., & Fosdick, L. S. (1939). The determination of halitosis by the use of the osmoscope and the cryoscopic method. *Journal of Dental Research, 18*(2), 127-32.

Brook, I. (1981). Aerobic and anaerobic bacterial flora of normal maxillary sinuses. *Laryngoscope, 91*(3), 372-376.

Burton, J., Chilcott, C., Moore, C., Speiser, G., & Tagg, J. (2006). A preliminary study of the effect of probiotic Streptococcus salivarius K12 on oral malodour parameters. *Journal of Applied Microbiology, 100*(4), 754-764. doi: 10.1111/j.1365-2672.2006.02837.x

Calil, C. M., & Marcondes, F. K. (2006). Influence of anxiety on the production of oral volatile sulfur compounds. *Life Sciences, 79*(7), 660-664. doi: 10.1016/j.lfs.2006.02.010

Carvalho, M. D., Tabchoury, C. M., Cury, J. A., Toledo, S., & Nogueira-Filho, G. R. (2004). Impact of mouthrinses on morning bad breath in healthy subjects. *Journal of Clinical Periodontology, 31*(2), 85-90. doi: 10.1111/j.0303-6979.2004.00452.x

Castellani, A. (1930). Foetor oris of tonsillar origin and certain bacilli causing it. *Lancet, 1*, 623-624.

Chapek, C. W., Reed, O. K., & Ratcliff, P. A. (1994). Management of periodontitis with oral-care products. *Compendium of Continued Education in Dentistry, 15*(6), 740-746.

Chapek, C. W., Reed, O. K., & Ratcliff, P. A. (1995). Reduction of bleeding on probing by oral care products. *Compendium of Continued Education in Dentistry, 16*(2), 188-196.

Claycomb, C. K. (1986). Malodors of the mouth. *Journal of the Oregon Dental Association*, 34-35.

Codipilly, D. P., Kaufman, H. W., & Kleinberg, I. (2004). Use of a novel group of oral malodor measurements to evaluate an anti-oral malodor mouthrinse (TriOralTM) in humans. *Journal of Clinical Dentistry, 15*(4), 98-104.

Cooke, M. (2003). Time profile of putrescine, cadaverine, indole and skatole in human saliva. *Archives of Oral Biology, 48*(4), 323-327. doi: 10.1016/S0003-9969(03)00015-3

Dawes, C. (1972). Circadian rhythms in human salivary flow rate and composition. *Journal of Physiology, 220*(3), 529-545.

De Boever, E., De Uzeda, M., & Loesche, W. (1994). Relationship between volatile sulfur compounds, BANA-hydrolyzing bacteria and gingival health in patients with and without complaints of oral malodor. *Journal of Clinical Denistry, 4*(4), 114-119.

De Boever, E. H., & Loesche, W. J. (1995). Assessing the contribution of anaerobic microflora of the tongue to oral malodor. *Journal of the American Dental Association, 126*(10), 1384-1393.

Doruk, C., Öztürk, F., Özdemir, H., & Nalçaci, R. (2008). Oral and Nasal Malodor In Patients With and Without Cleft Lip and Palate Who Had Undergone Orthodontic Therapy. *The Cleft Palate-Craniofacial Journal, 45*(5), 481-484. doi: 10.1597/07-074.1

Durham, T. M., Malloy, T., & Hodges, E. D. (1993). Halitosis: Knowing when "bad breath" signals systemic disease. *Geriatrics, 48*(8), 55-59.

Ede Tolentino, S., Chinellato, L. E., & Tarzia, O. (2011). Saliva and tongue coating pH before and after use of mouthwashes and relationship with parameters of halitosis. *Journal of Applied Oral Science, 19*(2), 90-94.

Eli, I., Baht, R., Koriat, H., & Rosenberg, M. (2001). Self-Perception Of Breath Odor. *Journal of the American Dental Association (1939), 132*(5), 621-626.

Erovic Ademovski, S., Lingstrom, P., Winkel, E., Tangerman, A., Persson, G. R., & Renvert, S. (2011). Comparison of different treatment modalities for oral halitosis. *Acta Odontologica Scandinavica, 70*(3), 224-233.

Farrell, S., Baker, R. A., Somogyi-Mann, M., Witt, J. J., & Gerlach, R. W. (2006). Oral malodor reduction by a combination of chemotherapeutical and mechanical treatments. *Clinical Oral Investigations, 10*(2), 157-163. doi: 10.1007/s00784-006-0044-5

Faveri, M., Hayacibara, M. F., Cancine Pupio, G., Cury, J. A., Ota Tsuzuki, C., & Hayacibara, R. M. (2006). A cross-over study on the effect of various therapeutic approaches to morning breath odour. *Journal of Clinical Periodontology, 33*(8), 555-560. doi: 10.1111/j.1600-051X.2006.00955.x

Figueiredo, L. C., Rosetti, E. P., Marcantonio, E., Marcantonio, R. C., & Salvador, S. L. (2002). The Relationship of Oral Malodor in Patients With or Without Periodontal Disease. *Journal of Periodontology, 73*(11), 1338-1342. doi: 10.1902/jop.2002.73.11.1338

Finkelstein, Y., Talmi, Y. P., & Zohar, Y. (2004). Laser cryptology for the treatment of halitosis. *Otolaryngology Head and Neck Surgery, 131*(4), 372-377.

Fletcher, S. M., & Blair, P. A. (1988). Chronic hallitosis from tonsilloliths: A common etiology. *Journal of the Louisiana State Medical Society, 140*(6), 7-9.

Fosdick, L. S., & Piez, K. A. (1953). Chemical studies in periodontal disease. X. Pap. chromagraphic investigation putrefaction associated periodontitis. *Journal of Dental Research, 32*(1), 87-100.

Franscella, J., Gilbert, R. D., Fernandez, P., & Hendler, J. (2000). Efficacy of a chlorine dioxide-containing mouthrinse in oral malodor. *Compendium of Continuing Education in Dentistry, 21*(3), 241-244.

Furne, J., Majerus, G., Lenton, P., Springfield, J., Levitt, D., & Levitt, M. (2002). Comparison of Volatile Sulfur Compound Concentrations Measured with a Sulfide Detector vs. Gas Chromatography. *Journal of Dental Research, 81*(2), 140-143. doi: 10.1177/154405910208100211

Ghyselen, J., Feenstra, L., & Van Steenberghe, D. (1996). Experiences of a Belgian multidisciplinary breath odour clinic (D. Van Steenberghe & M. Rosenberg, Eds.). In G. Delanghe (Author), *Bad Breath a multidisciplinary approach* (pp. 199-208). Leuven: Leuven University Press.

Gochman, N., Meyer, R. K., Blackwell, R. Q., & Fosdick, L. S. (1959). The amino acid decarboxylase of salivary sediment. *Journal of Dental Research, 38*, 998-1003.

Goldberg, S., Kozlovsky, A., & Rosenberg, M. (1995). Association of diamines with oral malodor (M. Rosenberg, Ed.). In *Bad breath: Research perspectives* (pp. 71-85). Tel Aviv: Tel Aviv University.

Goldberg, S., Kozlovsky, A., Gordon, D., Gelernter, I., Sintov, A., & Rosenberg, M. (1994). Cadaverine as a putative component of oral malodor. *Journal of Dental Research, 73*(6), 1176-1181.

Gordon, S. M., Szidon, J. P., Krotosznyski, B. K., Gibbons, R. D., & O'Neill, H. J. (1985). Volatile organic compounds in exhaled air from patients with lung chancer. *Clincal Chemistry, 31*(8), 1278-1282.

Grapp, G. (1933). Fetor oris (halitosis): A medical and dental responsbility. *Northwest Medical, 32*, 375-380.

Greenman, J., Duffield, J., Spencer, P., Rosenberg, M., Corry, D., Saad, S., ... El-Maaytah, M. (2004). Study on the Organoleptic Intensity Scale for Measuring Oral Malodor. *Journal of Dental Research, 83*(1), 81-85. doi: 10.1177/154405910408300116

Greenstein, R. B., Goldberg, S., Marku-Cohen, S., Sterer, N., & Rosenberg, M. (1997). Reduction of oral malodor by oxidizing lozenges. *Journal of Periodontology, 68*(12), 1176-1181.

Gross, A., Barnes, G., & Lyon, T. (1975). The effects of tongue brushing on tongue coating and dental plaque sores. *Journal of Dental Research, 54*(6), 1236.

Haraszthy, V., Zmabon, J., Sreenivasan, P., Zambon, M., Gerber, D., Rego, R., & Parker, C. (2007). Identification of oral bacterial species associated with halitosis. *Journal of the American Dental Association, 138*(8), 1113-1120.

Hartley, M. G., El Maaytah, M. A., McKenzie, C., & Greenman, J. (1996). The tongue microbiota of low odour and malodourous individuals. *Microbial Ecology in Health and Disease, 9*, 215-223.

Hu, D., Zhang, Y., Petrone, M., Volpe, A., DeVizio, W., & Giniger, M. (2005). Clinical effectiveness of a triclosan/copolymer/sodium fluoride dentifrice in controlling oral malodor: A 3-week clinical trial. *Oral Diseases, 11*(S1), 51-53. doi: 10.1111/j.1601-0825.2005.01091.x

Hunter, C., Niles, H., Vazquez, J., Kloos, C., Subramanyam, R., Williams, M., ... Majerus, G. (2005). Breath odor evaluation by detection of volatile sulfur compounds - correlation with organoleptic odor ratings. *Oral Diseases, 11*(S1), 48-50. doi: 10.1111/j.1601-0825.2005.01090.x

Iwanicka-Grzegorek, K., Lipkowska, E., Kepa, J., Michalik, J., & Wierzbicka, M. (2005). Comparison of ninhydrin method of detecting amine compounds with other methods of halitosis detection. *Oral Diseases, 11*(S1), 37-39. doi: 10.1111/j.1601-0825.2005.01087.x

Iwu, C. O., & Akpata, O. (1990). Delusional Halitosis. Review of the literature and analysis of 32 cases. *British Dental Journal, 168*(7), 294-296.

Johnson, B. E. (1992). Halitosis, or the meaning of bad breath. *Journal of General Internal Medicine, 7*(6), 649-656. doi: 10.1007/BF02599209

Kara, C., Tezel, A., & Orbak, R. (2006). Effect of oral hygiene instruction and scaling on oral malodour in a population of Turkish children with gingival inflammation. *International Journal of Paediatric Dentistry, 16*(6), 399-404. doi: 10.1111/j.1365-263X.2006.00769.x

Kato, H., Yoshida, A., Awano, S., Ansai, T., & Takehara, T. (2005). Quantitative detection of volatile sulfur compound- producing microorganisms in oral specimens using real-time PCR. *Oral Diseases, 11*(S1), 67-71. doi: 10.1111/j.1601-0825.2005.01096.x

Kazor, C. E., Mitchell, P. M., Lee, A. M., Stokes, L. N., Loesche, W. J., Dewhirst, F. E., & Paster, B. J. (2003). Diversity of Bacterial Populations on the Tongue Dorsa of Patients with Halitosis and Healthy Patients. *Journal of Clinical Microbiology, 41*(2), 558-563. doi: 10.1128/JCM.41.2.558-563.2003

Keller, M. K., Bardow, A., Jensdottir, T., Lykkeaa, J., & Twetman, S. (2011). Effect of chewing gums containing the probiotic bacterium Lactobacillus reuteri on oral malodour. *Acta Odontologica Scandinavica, 70*(3), 246-250.

Kiger, J. R., Brenkert, T. E., & Losek, J. D. (2008). Nasal Foreign Body Removal in Children. *Pediatric Emergency Care, 24*(11), 785-792. doi: 10.1097/PEC.0b013e31818c2cb9

Kim, J., Jung, Y., Park, K., & Park, J. (2009). A digital tongue imaging system for tongue coating evaluation in patients with oral malodour. *Oral Diseases*. doi: 10.1111/j.1601-0825.2009.01592.x

Kizhner, V., Xu, D., & Krespi, Y. P. (2011). A new tool measuring oral malodor quality of life. *European Archive of Otorhinolaryngology, 268*(8), 1227-1232.

Kleinberg, I., & Codipilly, D. M. (1997). The biological basis of oral malodor formation. In M. Rosenberg (Ed.), *Bad breath: Research perspectives* (pp. 13-39). Tel Aviv: Ramot Publishing Tel Aviv University.

Kleinberg, I., & Codipilly, D. M. (2002). Cysteinechallenge testing: A powerful tool for examining oral malodour processes and treatments in vivo. *International Dental Journal, 52*(S3), 221-228.

Kleinberg, I., & Westbay, G. (1992). Salivary and metabolic factors involved in oral malodor formation. *Journal of Periodontology, 63*(9), 768-775.

Kleinberg, I., Wolff, M. S., & Codipilly, D. M. (2002). Role of saliva in oral dryness, oral feel and oral malodour. *International Dental Journal, 52*(Suppl 3), 236-240.

Knaan, T., Cohen, D., & Rosenberg, M. (2005). Predicting bad breath in the non-complaining population. *Oral Diseases, 11*(S1), 105-106. doi: 10.1111/j.1601-0825.2005.01105_23.x

Koshimune, S., Awano, S., Gohara, K., Kurihara, E., Ansai, T., & Takehara, T. (2003). Low salivary flow and volatile sulfur compounds in mouth air. *Oral Surgery, Oral Medicine, Oral Pathology, Oral Radiology & Endodontics, 96*(1), 38-41. doi: 10.1016/S1079-2104(03)00162-8

Kostelc, J. G., Preti, G., Zelson, P. R., Brauner and, L., & Baehni, P. (1984). Oral odors in early experimental gingivitis. *Journal of Periodontal Research, 19*(3), 303-312. doi: 10.1111/j.1600-0765.1984.tb00821.x

Kostelc, J. G., Preti, G., Zelson, P. R., Stoller, N. H., & Tonzetich, J. (1980). Salivary volatiles as indicators of periodontitis. *Journal of Periodontal Research, 15*(2), 185-192. doi: 10.1111/j.1600-0765.1980.tb00273.x

Kostelc, J. G., Zelson, P. R., Preti, G., & Tonzetich, J. (1981). Quantitative differences in volatiles from healthy mouths and mouths with periodontitis. *Clinical Chemistry, 27*(6), 842-845.

Kozlovsky, A., Goldberg, S., Natour, I., Rogatky-Gay, A., Gelernter, I., & Rosenberg, M. (1996). Efficacy of a 2-phase oil:water mouthrinse in controlling malodor, gingivitis, and plaque. *Journal of Periodontology, 67*(6), 577-582.

Kozlovsky, A., Gordon, D., Gelernter, I., Loesche, W. J., & Rosenberg, M. (1994). Correlation between the BANA test and oral malodor parameters. *Journal of Dental Research, 73*(5), 1036-1042.

Krause, K. K., Graham, G. S., Stoffers, K. W., & Dennis, M. A. (1989). *The effectiveness of chlorine dioxide in the barrier system.* Lecture presented at Thomas P. Hinnman Meeting, Atlanta, GA.

Kurata, H., Awano, S., Yoshida, A., Ansai, T., & Takehara, T. (2008). The prevalence of periodontopathogenic bacteria in saliva is linked to periodontal health status and oral malodour. *Journal of Medical Microbiology, 57*(5), 636-642. doi: 10.1099/jmm.0.47706-0

Liu, X. N., Shinada, K., Chen, X. C., Zhang, B. X., Yaegaki, K., & Kawaguchi, Y. (2006). Oral malodor-related parameters in the Chinese general population. *Journal of Clinical Periodontology, 33*(1), 31-36. doi: 10.1111/j.1600-051X.2005.00862.x

Lochner, C., & Stein, D. J. (2003). Olfactory reference syndrome: Diagnostic criteria and differential diagnosis. *Journal of Postgraduate Medicine, 49*(4), 328-331.

Loesche, W. J., & Kazor, C. (2002). Microbiology and treatment of halitosis. *Periodontology 2000, 28*(1), 256-279. doi: 10.1034/j.1600-0757.2002.280111.x

Loesche, W. J., Bretz, W. A., Kerschensteiner, D., Stoll, J., Socransky, S. S., Hujoel, P., & Lopatin, D. E. (1990). Development of a diagnostic test for anaerobic periodontal infections based on placque hydrolysis of benzoyl-DL-arginine-naphthylamide. *Journal of Clinical Microbiology, 28*(7), 1551-1559.

Mackay, R. J., McEntyre, C. J., Henderson, C., Lever, M., & George, P. M. (2011). Trimethylaminuria: Causes and diagnosis of a socially distressing condition. *Clinical Biochemistry Review, 32*(1), 33-43.

Mantilla Gomez, S., Danser, M. M., Sipos, P. M., Rowshani, B., Van der Velden, U., & Van der Weijden, G. A. (2001). Tongue coating and salivary bacterial counts in healthy/gingivitis subjects and periodontitis patients. *Journal of Clinical Periodontology, 28*(10), 970-978. doi: 10.1034/j.1600-051x.2001.028010970.x

McDowell, J. D., & Kassebaum, D. K. (1993). Diagnosing and treating halitosis. *Journal of the American Dental Assocation,* 55-64.

Mcnamara, T., Alexander, J., & Lee, M. (1972). The role of microorganisms in the production of oral malodor. *Oral Surgery, Oral Medicine, Oral Pathology, 34*(1), 41-48. doi: 10.1016/0030-4220(72)90271-X

Miyazaki, H., Sakao, S., Katoh, Y., & Takehara, T. (1995). Correlation between volatile sulphur compounds and certain oral health measurements in the general population. *Journal of Periodontology, 66*(8), 679-684.

Morita, M., & Wang, H. (2001). Relationship Between Sulcular Sulfide Level and Oral Malodor in Subjects With Periodontal Disease. *Journal of Periodontology, 72*(1), 79-84. doi: 10.1902/jop.2001.72.1.79

Morita, M., Musinski, D. L., & Wang, H. (2001). Assessment of newly developed tongue sulfide probe for detecting oral malodor. *Journal of Clinical Periodontology, 28*(5), 494-496. doi: 10.1034/j.1600-051x.2001.028005494.x

Murata, T., Rahardjo, A., Fujiyama, Y., Yamaga, T., Hanada, M., Yaegaki, K., & Miyazaki, H. (2006). Development of a Compact and Simple Gas Chromatography for Oral Malodor Measurement. *Journal of Periodontology, 77*(7), 1142-1147. doi: 10.1902/jop.2006.050388

Murata, T., Yamaga, T., Iida, T., Miyazaki, H., & Yaegaki, K. (2002). Classification and examination of halitosis. *International Dentistry Journal, 52*(Supp3), 181-186.

Nachnani, S. (2011). Oral malodor: Causes, assessment, and treatment. *Compendium of Continuing Education in Dentistry, 31*(1), 22-4-26-8, 30-1.

Nachnani, S., Majerus, G., Lenton, P., Hodges, J., & Magallanes, E. (2003). Effects of training on odor judges scoring intensity. *Oral Diseases, 11*(Supp1), 937-944.

Nalcaci, R., & Baran, I. (2008). Oral malodor and removable complete dentures in the elderly. *Oral Surgery, Oral Medicine, Oral Pathology, Oral*

Radiology, and Endodontology, 105(6), E5-E9. doi: 10.1016/j.tripleo.2008.02.016

Newby, E., Hickling, J., Hughes, F., Proskin, H., & Bosma, M. (2008). Control of oral malodour by dentifrices measured by gas chromatography. *Archives of Oral Biology, 53*, S19-S25. doi: 10.1016/S0003-9969(08)70005-0

Ng, W., & Tonzetich, J. (1984). Effect of hydrogen sulfide and methyl mercaptan on the permeability of oral mucosa. *Journal of Dental Research, 63*(7), 994-997.

Niles, H., Hunter, C., Vazquez, J., Williams, M., & Cummins, D. (2005). The clinical comparison of a triclosan/copolymer/fluoride dentifrice vs a breath-freshening dentifrice in reducing breath odor overnight: A crossover study. *Oral Diseases, 11*(S1), 54-56. doi: 10.1111/j.1601-0825.2005.01092.x

Nonaka, A., Tanaka, M., Anguri, H., Nagata, H., Kita, J., & Shizukuishi, S. (2005). Clinical assessment of oral malodor intensity expressed as absolute value using an electronic nose. *Oral Diseases, 11*(S1), 35-36. doi: 10.1111/j.1601-0825.2005.01086.x

O'Heihir, T. (1992, April 4). Ugh! What can we do about that awful morning mouth? *RDH Magazine, 4*(12).

Olshan, A. M., Kohut, B. E., Vincent, J. W., Borden, L. C., Delgado, N., Qaqish, J., ... McGuire, J. A. (2000). Clinical effectiveness of essential oil-containing dentifrices in controlling oral malodor. *American Journal of Dentistry, 13*, 18C-22C.

Outhouse, T. L. (2009). Mouthrinses for the treatment of halitosis. *Journal of Evidence-Based Medicine, 2*(2), 129-130. doi: 10.1111/j.1756-5391.2009.01027_2.x

Payne, D., Gordon, J. J., Nisbet, S., Karwal, R., & Bosma, M. L. (2011). A randomized clinical trial to assess control of oral malodor by a novel dentifrice containing 0.1%w/w o-cymen-5-ol, 0.6%w/w zinc chloride. *International Dental Journal, 61*(S3), 60-66.

Pedrazzi, V., Sato, S., De Mattos, M. C., Lara, E. G., & Panzeri, H. (2004). Tongue-Cleaning Methods: A Comparative Clinical Trial Employing a Toothbrush and a Tongue Scraper. *Journal of Periodontology, 75*(7), 1009-1012. doi: 10.1902/jop.2004.75.7.1009

Persson, S., Edlund, M., Claesson, R., & Carlsson, J. (1990). The formation of hydrogen sulfide and methyl mercaptan by oral bacteria. *Oral Microbiology and Immunology, 5*(4), 195-201. doi: 10.1111/j.1399-302X.1990.tb00645.x

Peruzzo, D. C., Jandiroba, P. B., & Nogueira Filho, G. R. (2007). Use of 0.1% chlorine dioxide to inhibit the formation of morning volatile sulphur compounds (VSC). *Brazilian Oral Research, 21*(1), 70-74. doi: 10.1590/S1806-83242007000100012

Pitts, G., Brogdon, C., Hu, L., Masurat, T., Pianotti, R., & Schumann, P. (1983). Mechanism of action of an antiseptic, anti-odor mouthwash. *Journal of Dental Research, 62*(6), 738-742.

Pitts, G., Pianotti, R., Feary, T. W., McGuiness, J., & Masurat, T. (1981). The in vivo effects of an antiseptic mouthwash on odor-producing microorganisms. *Journal of Dental Research, 60*(11), 1891-1896.

Queiroz, C. S., Hayacibara, M. F., Tabchoury, C. M., Marcondes, F. K., & Cury, J. A. (2002). Relationship between stressful situations, salivary flow rate and oral volatile sulfur-containing compounds. *European Journal of Oral Sciences, 110*(5), 337-340. doi: 10.1034/j.1600-0722.2002.21320.x

Quirynen, M., Avontroodt, P., Soers, C., Zhao, H., Pauwels, M., & Van Steenberghe, D. (2004). Impact of tongue cleansers on microbial load and taste. *Journal of Clinical Periodontology, 31*(7), 506-510. doi: 10.1111/j.0303-6979.2004.00507.x

Quirynen, M., Avontroodt, P., Soers, C., Zhao, H., Pauwels, M., Coucke, W., & Vanstreenberghe, D. (2002). The efficacy of amine fluoride/stannous fluoride in the suppression of morning breath odour. *Journal of Clinical Periodonotology, 29*(10), 944-954.

Quirynen, M., Dadamio, J., Van den Velde, S., De Smit, M., Dekeyser, C., Van Tornout, M., & Vandekerckhove, B. (2009). Characteristics of 2000 patients who visited a halitosis clinic. *Journal of Clinical Periodontology, 36*(11), 970-975. doi: 10.1111/j.1600-051X.2009.01478.x

Quirynen, M., Mongardini, C., & Vansteenberghe, D. (1998). The effect of a 1-stage full-mouth disinfection on an oral malodor and microbial colonization of the tongue in periodontitis. A pilot study. *Journal of Periodontology, 69*(3), 374-382.

Quirynen, M., Zhao, H., Avontroodt, P., Soers, C., Pauwels, M., Coucke, W., & Steenberghe, D. V. (2003). A Salivary Incubation Test for Evaluation of Oral Malodor: A Pilot Study. *Journal of Periodontology, 74*(7), 937-944. doi: 10.1902/jop.2003.74.7.937

Quirynen, M., Zhao, H., Soers, C., Dekeyser, C., Pauwels, M., Coucke, W., & Steenberghe, D. V. (2005). The Impact of Periodontal Therapy and the Adjunctive Effect of Antiseptics on Breath Odor-Related Outcome Variables: A Double-Blind Randomized Study. *Journal of Periodontology, 76*(5), 705-712. doi: 10.1902/jop.2005.76.5.705

Rassamee-masmaung, S., Sirikulsathean, A., Amornchat, C., Hirunrat, K., & Rojanapanthu, P. (2007). Effects of herbal mouthwash containing the pericarp extract of Garcinia mangostana L on halitosis, plaque and papillary bleeding index. *Journal of the International Academy of Periodonotology, 9*(1), 19-25.

Ratcliff, P., & Bolin, V. (1992). *CLO2/phosphate germicide vs. Actinobacillus Actinomycetemcomitans and Prophyromonas (bacteriodes) gingivalis.* Lecture presented at AADR Meeting.

Ratcliff, P., & Bolin, V. (1993). *Antimicrobial capacity of chlorine dioxide based toothpaste.* Lecture presented at IADR Meeting.

Ratcliff, P. A., & Bolin, V. (1987). *Germicidal effect of provodine-iodide and CLO2 on dental pathogens.* Lecture presented at AADR Meeting.

Richter, J. L. (1996). Diagnosis and treatment of halitosis. *Compendium of Continuing Education in Dentistry, 17*(4), quiz 388, 374-376.

Riggio, M., Lennon, A., Rolph, H., Hodge, P., Donaldson, A., Maxwell, A., & Bagg, J. (2008). Molecular identification of bacteria on the tongue dorsum of subjects with and without halitosis. *Oral Diseases, 14*(3), 251-258. doi: 10.1111/j.1601-0825.2007.01371.x

Rio, A. D., Franchi-Teixeira, A. R., & Nicola, E. D. (2008). Relationship between the presence of tonsilloliths and halitosis in patients with chronic gaseous tonsillitis. *British Dental Journal, 204*(2), E4-E4. doi: 10.1038/bdj.2007.1106

Roldán, S., Herrera, D., O'Connor, A., González, I., & Sanz, M. (2005). A Combined Therapeutic Approach to Manage Oral Halitosis: A 3-Month Prospective Case Series. *Journal of Periodontology, 76*(6), 1025-1033. doi: 10.1902/jop.2005.76.6.1025

Rosenberg, M., & McCulloch, C. A. (1992). Measurement of oral malodor: Current methods and furture prospects. *Journal of Periodontology, 63*(9), 776-782.

Rosenberg, M., & Scully, C. (2003). Halitosis. *Dent Update, 3.*

Rosenberg, M. (1994). First international workshop on oral malodor. *Journal of Dental Research, 73*(3), 586-589.

Rosenberg, M. (1996). Clinical assessment of bad breath: Current concepts. *Journal of the American Dental Association, 127*(4), 475-482.

Rosenberg, M. (1997). Experiences of an Israeli malodor clinic. In E. Leib (Author) & M. Rosenberg (Ed.), *Bad breath: Research perspectives* (pp. 137-148). Tel Aviv: Ramrot Publishing - Tel Aviv University.

Rosenberg, M. (2002). The science of bad breath. *Scientific American, 286*(4), 72-79.

Rosenberg, M., Gelenter, I., Barki, M., & Bar-Ness, R. (1992). Day-long reduction of oral malodor by a two-phase oil:water mouthrinse as compared to chlorhexidine and placebo rinses. *Journal of Periodontology, 63*(1), 39-43.

Rosenberg, M., Knaan, T., & Cohen, D. (2007). Association between bad breath, body mass index, and alcohol intake. *Journal of Dental Research, 86*(10), 997-1000.

Rosenberg, M., Kozlovsky, A., Gelernter, I., Cherniak, O., Gabbay, J., Baht, R., & Eli, I. (1995). Reliability of clinical parameters for predicting the outcome of oral malodor treatment. *Journal of Dental Research, 74*(9), 1577-1582.

Rosenberg, M., Kulkarni, G., Bosy, A., & McCulloch, C. A. (1991). Reproducibility and sensitivity of oral malodor measurements with a portable sulphide monitor. *Journal of Dental Research, 70*(11), 1436-1440.

Rosenberg, M., Septon, I., Eli, I., Bar-Ness, R., Gelernter, I., Brenner, S., & Gabbay, J. (1991b). Halitosis measurement by an industrial sulphide monitor. *Journal of Periodonotology, 62*(8), 487-489.

Rosenberg, M. (n.d.). Bad breath: Diagnosis and treatment. *University of Toronto Journal, 3*(2), 7-11.

Ross, B., Dadgostar, N., Bloom, M., & McKeown, L. (2009). The analysis of oral air using selected ion flow tube mass spectrometry in persons with and without a history of oral malodour. *International Journal of Dental Hygiene, 7*(2), 136-143. doi: 10.1111/j.1601-5037.2008.00316.x

Schmidt, N. F., & Tarbet, W. J. (1978). The effect of oral rinses on organoleptic mouth odor ratings and levels of volatile sulfur compounds. *Oral Surgery Oral Medicine Oral Pathology, 45*(6), 876-883.

Schmidt, N., Missan, S., Tarbet, W., & Cooper, A. (1978). The correlation between organoleptic mouth-odor ratings and levels of volatile sulfur compounds. *Oral Surgery, Oral Medicine, Oral Pathology, 45*(4), 560-567. doi: 10.1016/0030-4220(78)90037-3

Scully, C., Porter, S., & Greenamn, J. (1994). What to do about halitosis. *British Medical Journal, 308*, 217-218.

Seemann, R., Bizhang, M., Djamchidi, C., Kage, A., & Nachnani, S. (2006). The proportion of pseudo-halitosis patients in a multidisciplinary breath malodour consultation. *International Dental Journal, 56*(2), 77-81.

Seemann, R., Kison, A., Bizhang, M., & Zimmer, S. (2001a). Effectiveness of mechanical tongue cleaning on oral levels of volatile sulfur compounds. *Journal of the American Dental Association, 132*(9), quiz 1318, 1263-1267.

Seemann, R., Passek, G., Bizhang, M., & Zimmer, S. (2004). Reduction of oral levels of volatile sulfur compounds (VSC) by professional toothcleaning and oral hygiene instruction in non-halitosis patients. *Oral Health Preventive Dentistry, 2*(4), 397-401.

Seemann, R., Passek, G., Zimmer, S., & Roulet, J. F. (2001b). The effect of an oral hygiene program on oral levels of volatile sulfur compounds (VSC). *Journal of Clinical Dentistry, 12*(4), 104-107.

Shimura, M., Watanabe, S., Iwakura, M., Oshikiri, Y., Kusumoto, M., Ikawa, K., & Sakamoto, S. (1997). Correlation between measurements using a new halitosis monitor and organoleptic assessment. *Journal of Periodonotology, 68*(12), 1182-1185.

Shinada, K., Ueno, M., Konishi, C., Takehara, S., Yokoyama, S., Zaitsu, T., ... Kawaguchi, Y. (2010). Effects of a mouthwash with chlorine dioxide on oral malodor and salivary bacteria: A randomized placebo-controlled 7-day trial. *Trials, 11*(1), 14. doi: 10.1186/1745-6215-11-14

Shiota, T., & Kunkel, M. F., Jr. (1958). In vitro chemical and bacterial changes in saliva. *Journal of Dental Research, 37*(5), 780-787.

Ship, J. A. (2003). Diabetes and oral health: An overview. *Journal of the American Dental Association, 134*(Spec No), 4S-10S.

Silness, J., & Löe, H. (1964). Periodontal Disease in Pregnancy II. Correlation Between Oral Hygiene and Periodontal Condition. *Acta Odontologica Scandinavica, 22*(1), 121-135. doi: 10.3109/00016356408993968

Silveira, E. M., Plccinin, F. B., Gomes, S. C., Oppermann, R. V., & Rosing, C. K. (2012). Effectiveness of gingivitis treatment on the breath of chronic periodontitis patients. *Oral Health Preventive Dentistry, 10*(1), 93-100.

Sodor, B., Johansson, B., & Sodor, P. O. (2000). The relation between foetor ex ore, oral hygiene and periodontal disease. *Swedish Dental Journal, 24*(4), 73-82.

Solis Gafar, M. C., Fischer, T. J., & Gaffar, A. (1979). Instrumental evaluation of odor produced by specific oral microorganisms. *Journal of the Society of Cosmetic Chemists, 30*, 241-247.

Sopapornamorn, P., Ueno, M., Vachirarojpisan, T., Shinada, K., & Kawaguchi, Y. (2006). Association between oral malodor and measurements obtained using a new sulfide monitor. *Journal of Dentistry, 34*(10), 770-774. doi: 10.1016/j.jdent.2006.02.004

Stamou, E., Kozlovsky, A., & Rosenberg, M. (2005). Association between oral malodour and periodontal disease-related parameters in a population of 71 Israelis. *Oral Diseases, 11*(S1), 72-74. doi: 10.1111/j.1601-0825.2005.01097.x

Stedman, R. L. (1968). Chemical composition of tobacco and tobacco smoke. *Chemical Reviews, 68*(2), 153-207. doi: 10.1021/cr60252a002

Steenberghe, D. V., Avontroodt, P., Peeters, W., Pauwels, M., Coucke, W., Lijnen, A., & Quirynen, M. (2001). Effect of Different Mouthrinses on Morning Breath. *Journal of Periodontology, 72*(9), 1183-1191. doi: 10.1902/jop.2000.72.9.1183

Stein, M. B., Torgrud, L. J., & Walker, J. R. (2000). Social phobia symptoms, subtypes, and severity: Findings from a community survey. *Archive of General Psychiatry, 57*(11), 1046-1052.

Sterer, N., & Rosenberg, M. (2006). Streptococcus salivarius promotes mucin putrefaction and malodor production by Porphyromonas gingivalis. *Journal of Dental Research, 85*(10), 910-914.

Sterer N, & Rosenberg M. (2011) <u>Breath Odors</u>. Springer – Verlag Berlin, Heidelberg

Sterer, N., Nuas, S., Mizrahi, B., Goldenberg, C., Weiss, E., Domb, A., & Davidi, M. (2008). Oral malodor reduction by a palatal mucoadhesive tablet containing herbal formulation. *Journal of Dentistry, 36*(7), 535-539. doi: 10.1016/j.jdent.2008.04.001

Sterer, N., Shaharabany, M., & Rosenberg, M. (2009). B-Galactosidase activity and H2S production in an experimental oral biofilm. *Journal of Breath Research, 3*, 4pp.

Suarez, F., Furne, J., Springfield, J., & Levitt, M. (2000). Morning Breath Odor: Influence of Treatments on Sulfur Gases. *Journal of Dental Research, 79*(10), 1773-1777. doi: 10.1177/00220345000790100701

Suarez, F., Springfield, J., Furne, J., & Levitt, M. (1999). Differentiation of mouth versus gut as site of orogin of odoriferous breath gases after garlic ingestion. *American Journal of Physiology, 276*(2 Pt 1), G425-G430.

Sulser, G. F., Brening, R. H., & Fosdick, L. S. (1939). Some conditions that effect the odor concentration of breath. *Journal of Dental Research, 18*(4), 355-359.

Tanaka, M., Anguri, H., Nishida, N., Ojima, M., Nagata, H., & Shizukuishi, S. (2003). Reliability of Clinical Parameters for Predicting the Outcome of Oral Malodor Treatment. *Journal of Dental Research, 82*(7), 518-522. doi: 10.1177/154405910308200706

Tanaka, M., Yamamoto, Y., Kuboniwa, M., Nonaka, A., Nishida, N., Maeda, K., ... Shizukuishi, S. (2004). Contribution of periodontal pathogens on tongue dorsa analyzed with real-time PCR to oral malodor. *Microbes and Infection, 6*(12), 1078-1083. doi: 10.1016/j.micinf.2004.05.021

Tangerman, A., & Winkell, E. (2007). Intra- and extra-oral halitosis: Finding of a new form of extra-oral blood-borne halitosis caused by dimethyl sulphide. *Primary Dental Care, 15*(2), 70-70. doi: 10.1308/135576108784000177

Tangerman, A. (2002). Halitosis in medicine: A review. *International Dental Journal, 52*(S3), 201-206.

Tangerman, A., Winkel, E. G., De Laat, L., Van Oiljen, A. H., & De Boer, W. A. (2012). Halitosis and helicobacter pylori infection. *Journal of Breath Research, 6*(1).

Terezhalmay, G. T., Gagliari, V. B., & Rybicki, L. A. (1994). Clinical evaluation of the efficacy and safety of the Ultrasonex ultrasonic toothbrush: A 30-day study. *Compendium of Continuing Dental Education, 15*(7), 866-874.

Tessier, J. F., & Kulkarni, G. V. (1991). Bad breath: Etiology, diagnosis, and treatment. *Oral Health*, 19-24.

Tonzetich, J., & Carpenter, P. (1971). Production of volatile sulphur compounds from cysteine, cystine and methionine by human dental plaque. *Archives of Oral Biology, 16*(6), 599-607. doi: 10.1016/0003-9969(71)90063-X

Tonzetich, J., & Ng, S. (1976). Reduction of malodor by oral cleansing procedures. *Oral Surgery, Oral Medicine, Oral Pathology, 42*(2), 172-181. doi: 10.1016/0030-4220(76)90121-3

Tonzetich, J., & Richter, V. (1964). Evaluation of volatile odoriferous components of saliva. *Archives of Oral Biology, 9*(1), 39-45. doi: 10.1016/0003-9969(64)90042-1

Tonzetich, J. (1971). Direct gas chromatographic analysis of sulphur compounds in mouth air in man. *Archives of Oral Biology, 16*(6), 587-597. doi: 10.1016/0003-9969(71)90062-8

Tonzetich, J. (1977). Production and Origin of Oral Malodor: A Review of Mechanisms and Methods of Analysis*. *Journal of Periodontology, 48*(1), 13-20. doi: 10.1902/jop.1977.48.1.13

Touyz, L. Z. (1993). Oral malodor - a review. *Journal of the Canadian Dental Association, 59*(7), 607-610.

Tsai, C., Chou, H., Wu, T., Yang, Y., Ho, K., Wu, Y., & Ho, Y. (2008). The levels of volatile sulfur compounds in mouth air from patients with chronic periodontitis. *Journal of Periodontal Research, 43*(2), 186-193. doi: 10.1111/j.1600-0765.2007.01011.x

Van den Velde, S., Quirynen, M., Van hee, P., & Van Steenberghe, D. (2007). Halitosis associated volatiles in breath of healthy subjects. *Journal of Chromatography B, 853*(1-2), 54-61. doi: 10.1016/j.jchromb.2007.02.048

Van den Velde, S., Van Steenberghe, D., Van Hee, P., & Quirynen, M. (2009). Detection of odorous compounds in breath. *Journal of Dental Research, 88*(3), 285-289.

Vandekerckhove, B., Van den Velde, S., De Smit, M., Dadamio, J., Teughels, W., Van Tornout, M., & Quirynen, M. (2009). Clinical reliability of non-organoleptic oral malodour measurements. *Journal of Clinical Periodontology, 36*(11), 964-969. doi: 10.1111/j.1600-051X.2009.01473.x

Videbech, T. (1966). Chronic olfactory paranoid syndromes. *Acta Psychiatrica Scandinavica, 42*(2), 183-213.

Wang, J., He, L., & Liu, T. T. (2012). Study on self-reported halitosis and the associated factors in patients in a periodontal clinic. *Bejing Da Xue Xue Bao, 44*(2), 295-298.

Washio, J. (2005). Hydrogen sulfide-producing bacteria in tongue biofilm and their relationship with oral malodour. *Journal of Medical Microbiology, 54*(9), 889-895. doi: 10.1099/jmm.0.46118-0

Watt, D. L., Rosenfolder, C., & Sutton, C. D. (1993). The effect of oral irrigation with a magnetic water treatment device on plaque and calculus. *Journal of Clinical Periodontology, 20*, 314-317.

Wigger-Alberti, W., Gysen, K., Axmann, E., & Wilhelm, K. (2010). Efficacy of a new mouthrinse formulation on the reduction of oral malodor A randomized, double-blind, placebo-controlled, 3 week clinical study. *Journal of Breath Research, 4*(1), 017102. doi: 10.1088/1752-7155/4/1/017102

Wilhelm, D., Himmelmann, A., Axmann, E. M., & Wilhelm, K. P. (2012). Clincical efficacy of a new tooth and tongue gel applied with a tongue cleaner in reducing oral halitosis. *Quintessence International, 43*(8), 709-718.

Wåler, S. M. (1997). The Effect of Zinc-Containing Chewing Gum on Volatile Sulfur-Containing Compounds in the Oral Cavity. *Acta Odontologica Scandinavica, 55*(3), 198-200. doi: 10.3109/00016359709115416

Wåler, S. M. (1997). On the transformation of sulfur-containing amino acids and peptides to volatile sulfur compounds (VSC) in the human mouth. *European Journal of Oral Sciences, 105*(5), 534-537. doi: 10.1111/j.1600-0722.1997.tb00241.x

Wozniak, W. (2005). The ADA guidelines on oral malodor products. *Oral Diseases, 11*(S1), 7-9. doi: 10.1111/j.1601-0825.2005.01080.x

Yaegaki, K., & Coil, J. M. (1999). Clinical dilemmas posed by patients with psychosomatic halitosis. *Quintessence International, 30*(5), 328-333.

Yaegaki, K., & Coil, J. M. (2000). Examination, classification, and treatment of halitosis; clinical perspectives. *Journal of the Canadian Dental Association, 66*(5), 257-261.

Yaegaki, K., & Sanada, K. (1992). Effects of a two-phase oil-water mouthwash on halitosis. *Clinical Preventive Dentistry, 14*(1), 5-9.

Yaegaki, K., & Sanada, K. (1992). Volatile sulfur compounds in mouth air from clinically healthy subjects and patients with periodontal disease. *Journal of Periodontal Research, 27*(4), 233-238. doi: 10.1111/j.1600-0765.1992.tb01673.x

Yaegaki, K., & Sanada, K. (1992b). Biochemcial and clinical factors influencing oral malodor in periodontal patients. *Journal of Periodontology, 63*(9), 783-789.

Yaegaki, K., Coil, J. M., Kamemizu, T., & Miyazaki, H. (2002). Tongue brushing and mouth rinsing as basic treatment measures for halitosis. *International Dental Journal, 52*(S3), 192-196.

Young, A., Jonski, G., & Rolla, G. (2003). Combined effect of zinc ions and cationic antibacterial agents on intraoral volatile sulphur compounds (VSC). *International Dental Journal, 53*(4), 237-242.

Zaleweska, A., Zatonski, M., Jablonka-Strom, A., Paradowsky, A., Kawala, B., & Litwin, A. (2012). Halitosis--a common medical and social problem. A review on pathology, diagnosis, and treatment. *Acta Gastro-enterologica Belgica, 75*(3), 300-309.

Zeng, Q. C., Wu, A. Z., & Pika, J. (2010). The effect of green tea extract on the removal of sulfur-containing oral malodor volatiles in vitro and its potential application in chewing gum. *Journal of Breath Research, 4*(3).

APPENDIX B
TESTIMONIALS

Many of the people I see have come to the National Breath Center as the last resort on a long journey to eliminate their bad breath and resume a normal life. My purpose in including these testimonials is to let those with chronic, severe bad breath know that *no matter what they have tried, no matter how long it's been there, and no matter how severe their bad breath is, there is an answer.*

From a Haitian woman who had been looking for a cure for many years:

"How does one even begin to tell their experiences with chronic Halitosis for some 35 years? I am now in my Fifties and until now I have been on a quest for a cure for this monster. All my working life I have worked in customer related jobs, still do; and can you imagine the stress knowing you are having this problem that nothing you tried has eliminated the problem till now. Thanks Dr. Richard Miller.

My journey to this point has been a silent nightmare. The day it really hit home was when my daughter, then three years old, yelled out at a party, Mummy your mouth smell like pooh. Imagine being at a high profile function and everyone turns to look at you. This is only one of the many embarrassing moments

I have encountered. So often I have been handed gum and heard others comment and laugh at me.

So many avoid me at work, functions, just about everywhere and I mean friends and family too. People will get up from beside you to find other seats or make excuses to leave the space I inhabited. Often I would hear an exclamation about whether someone has passed gas, or something smells like its rotting flesh, or it smell like a dirty diaper in here, or just it smells like pooh in here. Co-workers would have a field day saying things unpleasant and laughing. Like she is so pretty and her mouth is so stinky. I won't belabor you with all the agony I have experienced as you must get my plight by now.

How did I cope? Well I told myself I have done everything I could to take care of the issue to no avail but I will hopefully someday find a cure. Was this easy? No, but I try to avoid being in other people's space as much as I could and when I do, I speak very little. I have done/tried just about every dental work, physician care I possible could to take care of this problem. The truth is I have spent all my money just trying to deal with this issue. I even joked with one dentist that they say you can't take your money with you when you die and I said I am taking mine in my mouth. The truth is that I have exhausted funds, will-power and at one point in time I did not feel I wanted to live. When the people closest to you avoid you and make fun of you or even embarrass you, you really don't want to live. I am not saying there is no empathy but to hear a loved one talk about "bagging their head" to be in close contact with you and not being able to have a relationship with the opposite sex because they too say things and avoid you, that is more than anyone can endure.

Dr. Richard Miller is my angel and I mean he is. He is not only the answer to the cure of Halitosis, he is dedicated and kind along with his staff. For the first time I was comfortable and felt accepted in a medical environment. To those who are experiencing this nightmare, please, please do not spend another dime with doctors/dentist or anyone else. They do not have the answer. Take it from me, I want to help you from the ill faith I have experienced. I BEG YOU!! Again, take it from me, my Halitosis measured 560 when I went in to see Dr. Miller with the maximum being 1999 on the scale. That's how rotten eggs smell, he said. I broke down in tears just hearing that and with the feeling of trepidation that this may be another false offer to eliminate my problem, along with the fact I am so broke and I would not be able to afford the treatment. With my credit rating I had no way to make the payment and I was a mess internally but I was determined to give this a try. So I left the office with the figure to start the treatment, a decline application from Care Credit in hand and a guarantee that the treatment works.

Driving back to work, all that was going on in my mind is how I was going to come up with the funds. I have never asked anyone to help me financially but I was faced with my only possible chance, to once and for all cure this problem. So I thought of all those I have helped for an answer but could not broach the subject with them and so I called my daughter to use her credit. Needless to say she flipped and had to interview me that brought me to tears again. All I could think is how I sacrificed for my children but she came around and did what was necessary to get the funds. The next day I was scheduling my first appointment with Dr. Miller. The first available date was for the following week which seem like a decade away to me.

Treatment day one was painless and encouraging as there was a remarkable difference in the way my mouth tasted after the treatment. I have had that bad taste for so long. The bad taste in the back of my throat was gone after one treatment. I kept my visits regular and I am a few treatments away from my full treatment but I am CURED and everyone is accepting my company now. My self-esteem is coming back and I am more and more taking part in conversations.

Thanks Dr. Richard Miller and staff for your dedication to the cause that others neglect or refuse to make their patients know that there is truly a CURE out there for Halitosis. I only wish I could put a face to this message so you can all know that this is not a farce but truly a cure. Maybe someday I will, but I will voice this message to anyone I can to help the cause. If this is any consolation to the truth, remember I went broke in my quest to

be cured. Take the leap and see Dr. Richard Miller at the
National Breath Center; you will not regret it.

Thanks Doctor for your work and kindness and for giving me
back my life after thirty five years."

Leila K.

From a patient who was separated because of her bad
breath.

My husband first brought up the issue with my breath when we
were first dating. I spoke with my dentist, and he couldn't find
any issues. I asked several trusted friends about it, and they all
said they never noticed anything (with the exception of my sister,
who occasionally spelled something reminiscent from when I had
oral surgery when I was in high school.) I just figured I needed
to be a little more diligent--brush a little more often, make sure I
go to the dentist regularly, etc.

Many years went by, and the issue came up a few times. I
thought: maybe there was something stuck in my teeth. Maybe I
didn't get far enough back on my tongue when I brushed this
morning. Maybe I ate garlic today. Again, I just figured I needed
to be more diligent. Besides, I didn't really know what else to do!

It came to a head about a year ago with my husband, who was
tired of it cropping up so frequently. I went to the dentist again
(different dentist), and she didn't notice any issues.

Because it had become a more serious issue with my husband, I
knew I couldn't just stop there. I started doing some of my own
internet research. This was more confusing than helpful. For
anything that one person said, there were at least three people
who said it was the exact opposite. Use a tongue scraper. No
don't. It's usually your stomach. No, it's usually your
sinuses. No, it's always your tongue. Try this remedy. No, try

that one. It was very frustrating. I spoke with my general practitioner, who referred me to an ENT. The ENT referred me back to my dentist. AARGH! Part of the problem with the internet research is so much of it is from blogs, where anyone can make whatever claim they want without any sort of scientific backing.

Finally it hit me that in a city like DC, there was probably a specialist just for this. I did some more targeted internet research, and found Dr. Miller. I got his book, and it was very helpful. It was based on research with everything laid out very methodically. After the holidays, I made an appointment. Soon after, I began treatment.

I'll admit, the treatments were not painful, but they were a commitment. However, they worked! Within three months, my husband, Dr. Miller, and my sister could no longer detect an odor.

It has been over 1 year since the end of my treatment and I still have no issues. The ongoing regimen seemed a lot at first, but the cleaning routine became easier, particularly knowing it was preventing bad breath from returning.

In a few months we went from not knowing what to do to finding a complete cure.

Susan K.

From a woman from Kansas who traveled to see us.

Dear Dr. Miller,

You probably get a lot of positive comments but I just wanted to tell you how grateful I am.

I know you remember when I came in, I brought my boyfriend with me. He had been the first person to be honest about my breath. But he did more than that! He found you and the National Breath Center.

I was certainly skeptical when he told me, but after going through your most thorough diagnosis, when you told me how you could cure my halitosis, I was convinced. And, I was very glad that I could start the same day.

It's been over one and a half years since your treatment and I just want you to know that I have regained my confidence. I no longer dread meeting new people or being close to people. For me that alone is a life-changing event.

So, please know that you are appreciated for what you do at the Center. I am sure I am not the only one who has told you that but I just wanted you to know how my life has changed.

Deidre K.

APPENDIX C
MEDICATIONS RELATED TO HALITOSIS

OR CAUSING DRY MOUTH

A
Accutane
Actified
Adapin
Adipex-P
Adipost
Advil
Akineton
Aldomet
Anafranil
Anaspaz
Anaspaz PB
Anorex SR
Antivert
Aquatensin
Artane
Artane
Asendin
Atarax
Ativan
Atropisol
Atrovent
Aventyl

B
Banthine
Bellergal
Benadryl
Bentyl
Bontril PDM

C
Capoten
Catapres
Centrax
Chlor-Trimeton

Claritin
Clozaril
Cogentin
Comazine
Combid
Compazine
Comtrex
Coreg
Cytospaz
D
Daricon
Dalmane
Daxolin
Demerol
Diazide
Dimetane
Dimetapp
Dispal
Ditropan
Diuril
Dolobid
Donnatal
Dramamine
Dyazide

E
Elavil
Equanil
Esidrix
Eskalith

F
Fastin
Felbatol
Feldene
Fen-Phen

Flexeril

G

H
Halcion
Haldol
Hismanal
Historal
HydroDIURIL
Hygroton
Hyperoid

I
Ionamin
Imavate
Immodium AD
Inderal
Inderide
Inversine
Ismelin
Ispurel

J

K
Kinesed

L
Lamictal
Larodopa
Lasix
Librax
Librium
Lioresal
Lithane
Lithonate
Lomotil
Luvox

M
Marezine
Maxzide
Mazanor
Mellaril
Midamor
Miltown
Minipress
Moban
Moderatic
Motofen
Motrin
MS Contin

N
Nalfon
Naprosyn
Navane
Neurontin
Norflex
Norpramin

O
Orap
Ornade
P
Pamine
Parsidol
Pathibate
Paxil
Paxipam
Pertofrane
Phenergan
Phenran
Pondimin
Pro-Banthine
Proventil
Prozac
Pyribenzamine (PBZ)
Pyridium

Q
Quarzan

R
Rau-sed
Rautensin
Restoril

S
Sal-Tropine
Sanorex
Seldane
Serax
Serpasil
Sigequan
Sinemet
Sinequan
SK-Pramine
Sparine
Stelazine
Sudafed

T
Tegretol
Ten-Tab
Tenuate
Tepanil
Thorazine
Tofranil
Trac-Tabs
Transderm-Scop
Triaminic

U
Urispas

V
Valium

Ventolin
Vistaril
Vistrax
Vivactil

W
Wellbutrin
Wytensin

X
Xanax

Y

Z
Zantryl
Zoloft